Hazel Ant.

48703

BEHIND THE LINES

FROM NORTH AFRICA TO GERMANY

*Personal sketches of WW II,
taken from true stories
to his wife Esta*

MAJOR FREDRIC CONVERY,
A.U.S. (RET.)

FIRST EDITION

RED APPLE PUBLISHING
Peggy J. Meyer, editor/publisher
P. O. Box 101
Gig Harbor, WA 98335

Printed by Gorham Printing
Rochester, WA 98579

ISBN 1-880222-21-3

Library of Congress Catalog Card 95-67549

Cover & Page Design by Kathyrn E. Campbell

DEDICATION

*To my wife Esta
whose excellent support
made life better*

*Fred and Esta, July 1941,
Tacoma, Washington, after arriving at Ft. Lewis February 2.*

ACKNOWLEDGMENT

A special thank-you to
Roy W. Stonecypher
&

Roberta (Bobbie) Nelson
whose computer assistance was invaluable.

INTRODUCTION

Fredric Convery entered into his military service in 1921 going into the National Guard at the age of eighteen. In 1938 his wife died, having given him two sons, then age six and three, Richard and Robert.

Fred was inducted into military service in February 1941 for supposedly six months and had to leave the two boys in charge of a housekeeper. September 2 he married Esta. Ten days later he was shipped to Ft. Monroe, Virginia, for further military training. This left Esta with the immediate problem of raising and caring for two lively young boys.

The bombing of Pearl Harbor began World War II, and Fred was ordered to report to his Anti-Aircraft unit to guard an aircraft plant at Hawthorne, California. Esta closed the household and followed Fred to Hawthorne with the two boys in February of 1942. The new family moved whenever Fred was transferred to other military locations throughout the United States until April of 1943 when Fred's unit was shipped overseas to Algeria, North Africa. From that time on until September of 1945, when Fred came home from the war, she was alone in the raising of Dick and Bob. Through Esta's efforts helping Fred with his two young boys, both became well-adusted young men. Apparently, Esta did a good job because now in 1995, Dick is a highly respected medical doctor and professor at the University of California, San Diego, and Bob is a retired Test Flight Engineer from the Boeing Company in Seattle.

PREFACE

I was assigned to the 457th CA AA (Anti-Aircraft) Battalion as Executive Officer in the summer of 1942 and ordered to report to Camp Hulen, Palacious, Texas. The battalion formed there was in training with Lt. Colonel Clemens commanding. Before the battalion could be shipped out, it had to be inspected by a team that reviewed the facets of the training that had been completed. The inspection lasted two days.

In the afternoon of the first day, Col. Clemens ordered me to the obstacle course where all of the men were going through various obstacles. Previously, a group of four new 2nd lieutenants, fresh from Officers' Training School, had been sent to the obstacle course by Col. Clemens. An inspecting officer questioning the new officers about the training program discovered that they knew nothing about the procedures. I came up. I was asked to identify the ranking officer present. Of course, I had to reply that it was I. Nothing more was said. However, the next day the inspecting officer in charge ordered the withdrawal of my promotion papers to major, the reason being the very poor showing of the new 2nd lieutenants who knew nothing about the obstacle course. Col. Clemens offered no explanation. That was the first of a series of incidents affecting my promotion to major. A few days later I was transferred to the 439th AA Battalion and given command of Battery A. The 439th AA, after a brief period of training, moved to Hattiesburg. Mississippi, for further training until February 1943 when the battalion was sent to the port of embarkation at Camp Dix, New Jersey. The trip was not without incident. During the movement by train from Camp Shelby at Hattiesberg to Camp Dix, Major Edwin W. Jones, Executive Officer and train commander, became very drunk and raised a considerable amount of trouble with the train crew. One night about midnight, when the troop train had been on a siding for quite some time, Jones, irate over the delay, called a vice-president of the railroad and bitterly complained. Subsequently, he was court-martialed for his behavior.

The following writings are from stories I sent home during 28 months of WWII, spanning the period from April 1943 through August 1945. During that time my military life was spent going across Algeria and Tunisia in North Africa and across the Mediterranean to Italy. August 1944 took me on the landing and invasion of Southern France, north through France and into Germany in 1945.

DISCLAIMER . . . Every effort has been made to make this book of WWII sketches as accurate as possible. A few changes have been made to protect the rights of others. Because of censorship, my letters to my wife Esta could not contain any details of wartime activity—hence, the absence of warfare stories other than from diaries, personal letters, news items, articles from *Stars and Stripes Weekly*, individual battalion histories, and "The Roving Reporter" columns by Ernie Pyle. These were added to offer in-depth or alternative enhancement to the stories.

—Major Fredric Convery

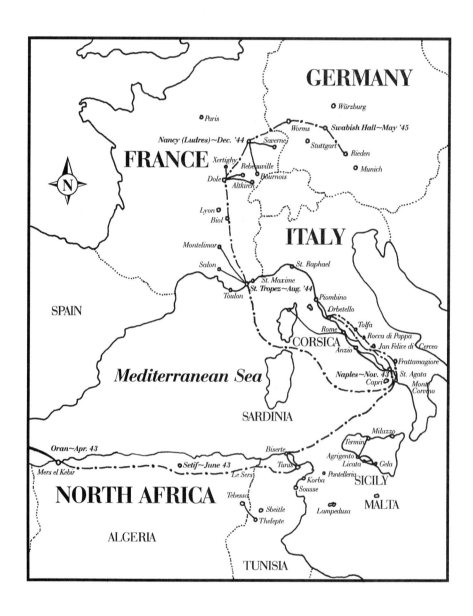

Map of European Theatre of War covered by Major Convery:
North Africa (Algeria and Tunisia), Italy, France, and Germany

CONTENTS

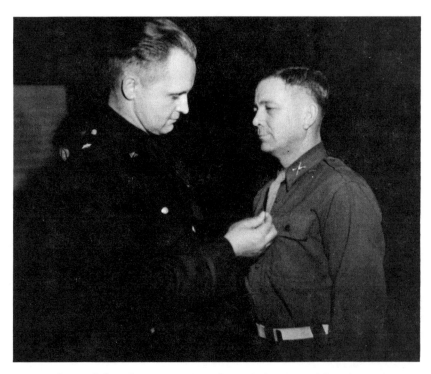

Fred Receiving the Bronze Star from Brig. Gen. Glen O. Barcus

PART I

ALGERIA

April 1943

The 439th AA Battalion arrived safely at Oran and in good shape. Everybody's money was picked up for exchange into francs and was not returned until about a week later.

Fred had spent five days in the hospital aboard ship with the flu and was back in the hospital in Oran with what the doctor called bronchial pneumonia. Nothing serious, but Captain Daily, the battalion medical officer, thought he would recover faster in the hospital.

The hospital was formerly a private hospital about 10 miles from camp. The building was very modern but not large. It had 7 stories but only 37 beds, all in private rooms. The first floor had been for offices; the second for the kitchen; the third, fourth, fifth, and sixth for the patients. The top floor was where two doctors had lived who were in charge of the hospital. The whole building was now for officers only.

The ambulance taking the Captain to the hospital had quite a time finding it because the whole town was a mass of unplanned streets, alleys and buildings. The ambulance driver went first to the regular enlisted men's hospital to get a guide. He had been there six or seven times, but was lost as soon as they started. It took 45 minutes to locate the place. There was only about a mile between the two hospitals. When the driver would go around a corner, turn around a block, or even turn around and come right back, the corner would be gone because of blind ends and curving streets.

There were English as well as American officers in the hospital. They were all quite cheerful. Lieutenant Fox, whose bed was next to the Captain's, was a very typical Englishman. He had a rather large reddish-brown mustache, although his hair was nearly black. His field artillery outfit had been shelled, and when a shell came close he had jumped into a foxhole. The shell exploded about 50 feet away. He was all the way into the foxhole except for his left hand which caught a piece of shrapnel. The doctors were having quite a time trying to save his hand because so many bones and muscles were broken and cut. Another officer was hit by a sniper and also had several pieces of shrapnel in his chest. Most of the men were going back to England before long. Nearly all those injured had been in infantry outfits.

One night Oran harbor had an air raid. This was Fred's introduction to the actual war, with air-raid sirens blaring, bombs hitting, and anti-aircraft tracer shells going up from all around the harbor. Everybody was ordered to the basement—patients, nurses and attendants. All jammed in with standing-room only. A very angry medical officer came in. One of the patients was sick with the mumps, and the medical officer was positive that every person in that basement was about to contract the disease.

Fred was released from the hospital and returned to the Battery campground, located on a high hill overlooking a beautiful valley. Farming in the valley was mostly vineyards that were operated by Arabs and a few French. The spoken languages were French, Arabic, and Spanish. The children were dirty and dressed just as you would imagine Arab children to be dressed. The Arabs wore turbans and short skirts even while they worked.

The Battery took a hike around the valley and through a village. No one lived on the farms; they all lived in the village. The houses were made from a sort of adobe brick and looked like

Southern California buildings with tile roofs. All had high walls, preventing a view of the yards. The stucco was either a real light yellow or a dark pinkish yellow. The children, all a bunch of beggars, would run alongside the trucks and jeeps saying "Gimme candy" or "Gimme chewgum" or "Gimme penny."

Rations included candy, razor blades and a few other items. The ration was plenty to take care of anyone—eight packages of cigarettes and from three to six candy bars per week.

About one-tenth of the people were Europeans, the rest being Arabs. The Arabs were great thieves and did not consider thievery an improper profession. Close watch had to be kept to stop them from getting into camp. The country was a lot like California, hot during the day but cool at night. Daytime was hotter than blazes, but being on a hill where there was a breeze helped to make the heat tolerable.

A woman was found in a grocery store who would do the officers' laundry, but when they went after the laundry, she hadn't done it because she had no soap. Soap was rationed. In order to get their laundry done, they had to go back to camp for soap. At the grocery store, one of the officers bought half a dozen lemons, six tomatoes, and about two pounds of string beans—costing 90 cents. The cook fixed them for the officers' mess and they feasted on fresh vegetables and real lemonade. That gave the Captain the idea to go out with a truck and buy enough fresh vegetables from some farmer for the whole Battery. He located the vegetables but didn't buy any. The beans were $6.00 for less than a bushel; tomatoes and lemons were $22.00 for a basket smaller than a half bushel. The farmers didn't want money because there was nothing to buy.

While he was looking for vegetables, he came across a little place where there was a butcher who was butchering a pair of sheep in the open—one sheep was already butchered and hanging in a tree, all covered with flies. The second was just being started. The Arab had bled it, cut the artery in the hind leg, and was blowing with his mouth into the artery. The sheep was all puffed up with air like a balloon, and the skin was tight. Then he beat the hide with a stick, loosening the skin. In fact, the whole process was to prepare the sheep for skinning.

★ ★ ★

By the end of April the weather was getting warmer, especially at night. Where two blankets and a sleeping bag had been used, it was too warm in just a sleeping bag. Sleeping under mosquito bar kept the flies out. The mosquitos had not been bad, but because the nights were getting warmer they began to show up. The mosquitos were the type that carried malaria and it was necessary to be careful. A yellow pill called *antebrin* was taken once a week. It combated malaria and had the same effect as quinine. The flies were vicious. They would bite right through your socks and had to be fought all the time with traps, screens and fly spray. Food was kept covered, and crude oil was put around the latrines. Those flies carried the germ that caused dysentery. One officer had dysentery so bad that he had to be transported to the hospital on a stretcher.

The men built a place to wash their clothes, and it worked quite well. They acquired an oil drum, cut one end out, and then filled it with soap and water for boiling their clothes. A table was built of scrap lumber with two washboards. The boys took a couple of planks, cut ridges in them with knives, and made, according to the boys from the South, a rub board. The whole arrangement was okay. However, there was not a close water supply, and all the water used had to be carried from about a quarter of a mile away. It was quite a job to keep 170 men clean, considering the bathing, drinking, cooking, and washing of mess gear, clothing and cooking utensils.

It was understood why canned foods were rationed in the States. Nearly everything came in cans, and the troops ate quite well. It was a wonder that they ate as well as they did. They did get some frozen meat and bread baked by mobile bakeries. Other than that, the food was all in cans—milk, vegetables, canned meats, fruits, cheese (better than in the States because it was not so green), and dehydrated onions that tasted like fresh ones when soaked in water. Dehydrated potatoes and powdered eggs helped to make donuts, hot cakes and French toast. When the supplies failed to come, eating was really monotonous. The water was heavily chlorinated and hard to drink. For meals, they had coffee or lemonade made with powder that also came in cans. Several kinds of soup were all good and tasted exactly as they should. A #10 can of dehydrated split pea, bean and vegetable soup material would make enough for 170 men. A tomato cocktail was dehydrated and seasoned just right. Canned grapefruit was also excellent.

★ ★ ★

Going into a barber shop for a haircut, shampoo and shave was quite an experience. Supposedly the shops were clean, according to local standards, but certainly not to American. The chairs were all quite old and did not tip back for the customers to lie flat. The barber had to half squat to do his work, and he also seemed to be in an awkward position for shaving. Instead of having an apron to throw over his customer, Fred was instructed to put on a coat in a backward arrangement, like a surgeon's coat. The chair was close to a washbasin, and after being shaved, the customer washed his own face. For washing hair, the barber went after warm water in the back of the shop and brought it out in a jug. The chairs were quite close together and did not swing around. Consequently, there were eight chairs in a shop that in America would have had about four. A hair cut, shampoo, and tonic cost 90 cents. The barber came right up to the cashier and held out his hand for the tip.

The Arab women with their faces showing were the single ones, and the ones with their faces covered were married. The story was passed around that whatever you do don't fool around with an Arab's woman. If you were caught, they would cut out your testicles and sew them up in your mouth.

The street cars were funny little things that had an extra open car that was towed along behind. They were always crowded with standing room only. The tracks ran on the side of the streets next to the curb.

Captain Convery visited a school for boys, ages six to nine, who were studying geography. The teacher could speak English and said the children wanted to thank the U.S. for the milk. He didn't know it, but the U.S. was sending powdered milk over for the Arab children. No business or cafe was allowed to sell milk; it was exclusively for the children. The powdered milk was mixed with water and tasted almost like fresh milk. Out in the park, Fred talked to a boy who was about eleven years old. He had had one year of English and could speak English very well.

★ ★ ★

In June, the Battalion moved and was located about two miles outside of a small village, much cleaner than Oran and with much more evidence of wealth. Fred went in to the village to make some arrangements about getting the laundry done for the men and saw a lot of interesting things around the town. The laundry was all hand-washed by French women who used wooden tubs and wooden washboards. The laundry was set up in what used to be a dairy barn, all concrete, right in the middle of the town. The wash water emptying into the gutters in the barn finally reached the gutter in the paved main street. The clothes were hung outside to dry, in what used to be the barnyard, and then brought back in for ironing. Women and girls did the ironing with old-fashioned irons heated over a charcoal stove. Soap had to be furnished, one bar for every ten pieces of clothing.

★ ★ ★

One day the whole Battery went for a swim in the sea. The Battery started out from camp at 8:30 a.m. and had to shuttle the men to the beach because only two trucks were available. The country looked like Eastern Washington but with a little more vegetation. A shrub, like sagebrush, grew in the rocky soil, only thicker and greener but about the same height. As they went down a narrow, winding, very steep road, they passed through an Arab village. It was built right up the mountain from the sea, and from a distance it looked like pictures of cliff dwellers. Getting closer, the houses became individual buildings. There were a number of goat herds but no cows. The goats made parallel trails on the hills that looked like contour lines on a map. The houses were all built of stone and stucco without a sign of lumber. There was absolutely no way to tell how long ago they had been built. The sea was a beautiful sight, the bluest water anyone had ever seen. The sky was without a cloud, and the sun was beating down. When Arab women saw the trucks coming, they would turn their backs, sort of pick up their clothing from their shoulders, and put it over their heads, fold it over their faces, and then turn to face the trucks with only one eye showing. One of them gave a half wave by using the hand that was not holding her face covering. She held her hand about halfway up and just bent her fingers. An Arab youngster said that the Germans took everything of value from the stores, drove away the cattle and sheep, and forced the Arab women to marry the German soldiers.

The mountains came straight down to the sea, as if water had been put around bare hills. There was a wonderful place to swim. The water was as clear as a bell and the sand very clean. There was not one bit of shade. The noon meal was brought over by truck. One boy who was tan all over forgot that he was not tanned on his rear. When they started for camp, he was still brown all over but with a brilliant pink bottom. They started back to camp with the first two truckloads at 4:00 p.m. There were no lights to use in the evening, and by 9:00 p.m. it was dark. In order to get eight hours' sleep while it was dark, they had to go to bed at 10:00 and get up at 6:00.

★ ★ ★

There were quite a number of beauty shops, *Coiffeur pour*

Dames. After noticing that there were so many, one began to look at the hair of the French women. None of them wore hats, and they must have had their hair fixed every day. It was piled high on their heads in a solid fashion, with deep wide waves and puffs that started at their foreheads and went down on the back of their necks. For certain, they could not fix those hairstyles themselves.

Arabs sold drinks out of a goat skin hung over the shoulder. The skin was sewn up, of course, to hold water. At one end, which stuck out from under the arm, there was a spigot affair. They carried two brass bowls, and everyone who bought a drink used one or the other of the two bowls. Needless to say, the only persons buying drinks from them were the Arabs. One evening about 5:30 an Army band came down the street on parade. They were playing and were followed by the Colors and a detachment of troops. Everyone always enjoyed parades, but this one, even though short, gave quite a thrill—way over there in North Africa. Of course, all the U.S. soldiers and sailors saluted the Colors, but the French civilians just removed their hats. The troops were black soldiers from some quartermaster outfit nearby and they were strutting their stuff, marching perfectly.

★ ★ ★

The Red Cross ran a cafe (no choice of food) for all ranks. Because there were so many wanting to eat, there was always a long waiting line, except for officers who did not need to wait. The food was really not too good. The Red Cross also maintained an Officers' Club with a large room for reading and resting. In the basement was a washroom and showers. To take care of hungry officers, there was a snack bar at which they served bread, butter, a spread, and food with which to make sandwiches—like Spam, jam, and canned salmon. Never anything different. There was usually something to drink—either cocoa, lemonade, or sometimes coffee. There was always a crowd. It was necessary to work your way in. When you did get something to eat, it tasted good. A sign above a box read "One franc if you think it is worth it."

One franc was two cents, and it was worth it. In the afternoon they served real American ice cream. There was a waiting line of about 150. By the time a small cup of ice cream was served, it was melted, but it still tasted good.

* * *

The Battalion moved again and was in a nicer place in the middle of a wheat field. The land was level and there was not half as much wind as there had been. The days were very hot and it was expected to get even hotter.

* * *

On the next move the officers really got a break because they were stationed in an old Foreign Legion post and were quite comfortable. There were a number of buildings that were built a long time ago with thick walls and tile roofs. There was also a British Officers' Club where they served Scotch whiskey by the drink, as well as beer and wine. It was the first place in Northern Africa that had sold anything but wine. The enlisted men did not have it too good because they were in a regular dust bowl.

* * *

Several officers made a trip to a monastery. They traveled over the same route that was taken by Battery A several weeks before. Going through a canyon, a large baboon crossed the road right in front of them. There seemed to be quite a number around that area. As they came out of the canyon, they took a side road and then followed a seldom-used road farther up the valley. The road was lined with olive trees, and closer to the road was a stone wall on either side. The road and rock work must have been there for quite some time because there was moss and other growth on the rock face. Moss was not abundant around there because of the arid conditions. When they finally got to the monastery, es-tablished forty years before, they found it to be a regular building, similar to other buildings around there, set in the midst of a group of utility buildings. The monks, not more than six or eight in number, belonged to the Order of White Fathers. The work was done mostly by Arabs and supervised by the monks. The Father Superior was a very pleasant individual who had kindness written all over his face. Another monk whom they met was equally pleasant. Both had black pointed beards that had a tendency to grow out rather than down. The Father Superior was dressed in a plain white robe and wore a white pith helmet. He showed them around the gardens and orchard. All kinds of vegetables were growing but none were for sale. Among the trees were several kinds of shade and fruit trees—apple, orange, lemon, tangerines, olive and pear.

Down the hill, where they made their wine, the building was quite modern in most respects but antiquated in others. Caves ran back into the hill where the wine was stored. The casks were rolled back on two rails. As the wine was sold, it was siphoned out of the large casks into smaller casks. To see in the back part, they used acetylene lamps such as miners used except that these were carried by a handle. At the innermost end of the cave, a cross cave was dug connecting to another. In between, off of the cross cave, were rooms in which the wine was stored in bottles, which were, in turn, piled inside the rooms and then covered with sand.

After sampling, some Vin Rouge was bought, a red wine, and some Vin Rosé, a light red wine. That which was bought was bottled in 1936, and by comparing to their ordinary wine, which had been made the year before, was far better. In the same building they had a grist mill and a saw mill.

★ ★ ★

The Battalion was assigned to guard a temporary airfield in a desert area near Setif, Algeria. The runways were not paved but had ribbon-like steel strips rolled out crosswise on the sand. Heavy planes could use the runway, but it was mainly used by fighter planes.

A B-17 bomber landed one day. The young pilot had flown the plane from the States and had become separated from the lead plane. Groups of planes were flown over with a lead plane doing the navigating and the rest of the planes following. When he spotted the airstrip, he landed to find out just where he was. After he found out, he took off for his final destination.

The field was used mainly by British Spitfires brought to the field for repairs from combat damage. A British maintenance squadron was based at the airfield. The guns of the Battalion were placed at various positions a mile or so out from the airstrip.

Because the gun crews had to stay at the gun sites around the clock, their meals had to be taken out to them. This worked out all right, but residing in the fields and desert is anything but livable without water. The solution to the problem was to get a water supply to the crews. Because there was no equipment to do this, Capt. Convery went over to the British Headquarters, located the supply officer and another officer in charge to see whether they had anything that could be used to keep the men supplied with water. They offered some gasoline drums that turned out to be just the right thing. Water could be hauled to the sites, and the crews could keep a supply on hand for their use. The supply officer and his friend said they were glad to be of assistance but asked a bit of trading in return. Convery said sure and asked what they needed. They were both anxious to have a pair of suntan slacks. The British uniform was shorts, and the two of them really wanted a pair of long pants. Fred was able to get a couple of pairs out of one of the supply rooms, and from that time on they were the best of friends.

Two British officers

A number of reciprocal trades were made, and each time it seemed the exchange was most beneficial to both parties. The British rations (all canned foods, as were ours) had no vegetables or fruit juices, mostly canned potatoes, beef, and hard thick crackers. As a consequence, with no vitamin C in their diet, the slightest scratch on their legs or arms from brush or anything else would soon start to fester. That was the reason they were so anxious for some slacks.

The British supply issues included a regular allowance of liquor, whiskies, gin, etc. The U.S. forces had no liquor allowances of any kind at that time of the war. It so happened that the British liked coffee for breakfast rather than tea, which they had for all meals. A trade was made of one pound of coffee and a can of grapefruit juice for a fifth of Johnny Walker Black Label Scotch. They were crazy for the juice and thought they had made the best deal.

While going through their warehouse, looking for anything that might be needed, Convery spotted some Perfection oil heaters. The heaters burned kerosene like a lamp, using a large round wick that fed kerosene from a round tank in the bottom of the heater. They let him have one to take back, and that was the most comforting item of Convery's personal possessions. It stayed with him all through the war.

One evening Capt. Convery was invited to the British officers' mess, which was in a French Foreign Legion building. The building had a barroom, which they had stocked abundantly. It was functioning very well. They all went into the bar and had a few drinks before dinner. Finally, Squadron Leader Howard, one of the two friends, asked Convery whether he would like to have the *office copy*. That was a new one. It meant *the last one before dinner*. Howard had been an employee of Lloyds Bank in London. On the way to the dining room, he tossed out another British expression. He said, "*Old chap, would you like to splash your boots?*" That was not understandable at all. What he meant was, "*Would you like to go to the latrine?*"

★ ★ ★

24

One afternoon Captain Kimmerer and Captain Daily asked Convery to go into Setif with them to shop around. They came across an Arab shoemaker who was making some sandals. He used the liners from tires for soles and native tanned leather for the uppers or tops. Convery bought three pair, one each for his wife Esta and sons Dick and Bob. He guessed at the sizes and thought that he had them just about right.

After he came home in 1945, Esta told him the sandals had a terrific odor. They could not be kept in the apartment. She hung them in the garage and left them there without being used or worn for two months, but still the odor was there and she had to throw them out. Subsequent to his shipping of the sandals, he learned that the native method of curing leather in Africa was to bury the leather in piles of camel manure for a considerable time.

Watering trough

Every village had a watering trough fed by a spring. All the natives went to the troughs for water and carried it away in various containers. There was a trough in front of the barn in which Headquarters was billeted. Horses, cows, sheep, etc. came in during the day. One evening an old woman came down and filled her goat skin. She put it on the ledge of the trough and then got under it and carried it off. She could not have weighed over 80 pounds, and the bag filled with water weighed about 60 pounds. The natives also had two-wheeled carts built with 50-gallon gasoline drums for hauling water from the trough. That was the Battalion's source of water, but because there were so many malaria cases the water was heavily chlorinated. The water was better without chlorine, but everyone would rather have tasted the chlorine than have a case of malaria. The water from the spring came out of a stone post that had a date of 1878.

Trips were made into Setif just to see what could be found in the stores that would be interesting. Those stores were certainly something different. One store was a small department store. Just try to imagine everything being sold out, no stock, and only a few things on two or three counters. They had some local metal polish, rag rugs, wooden toys, a few blankets, and miscellaneous odds and ends. When making a sale, the salesgirl took the sales slip and the customer to a cashier who then wrote down each item in a brown ledger. No cash register, just a cash drawer.

Money belts were not worn because it was just too hot. Being as warm and hot as it was, the belt made one sweat all the time. Anything tight did the same. It was a strange climate there. If clothes were loose, the perspiration dried fast enough so that it was not too uncomfortable. If anything was tight, the sweat accumulated. Those Arabs were smart with their loose clothing.

In Setif was what might be called a tailor shop area. On the sidewalk of one whole block were Arab tailors. Each one was working on a Singer sewing machine sewing Arab clothing. The sidewalk was covered by a building with arches along the curb. Each tailor had his own little work space between the arches. All were old men and each one had a beard. The street and sidewalks were filled with Arabs.

A jeep with two officers was going through the city. Out from the sidewalk ran an Arab boy, and because the jeep could not go very fast, he could run beside it. As he ran, he evidently was trying to sell something. He was saying, "Kap-i-tan, Kap-i-tan, zig-zig, champagne, sissy." He was drumming up business for some Arab gal.

★ ★ ★

While in the Setif area, one of the officers was able to obtain a butchered sheep. Fresh meat had not been available since arriving in Africa, and the thought of barbecued lamb seemed like something that called for a party. Nobody had ever barbecued any meat, but one of the officers said that his father had done a lot of barbecuing. He thought he knew what to do. At first, it was thought that there was going to be barbecued lamb, but as it later turned out, it was barbecued mutton.

A pit was dug about two feet deep and four feet long. At each end was support for a pipe that crossed over the pit, and the carcass of the sheep was fastened onto the pipe. The fire was built in the pit early in the day and the barbecuing was started. The carcass was turned regularly and everyone hoped that by evening the meat would be well done and tasty. In the evening, all the officers of the Battalion came to Headquarters (that is, those who were not on duty), and had some of the barbecued mutton. Captain Daily fixed up some of his Kickapoo juice with his alcohol, and they proceeded to have a good party. Kickapoo juice was lemonade concentrate (sugar and lemon juice), water, and pure grain alcohol. It was considered a military secret.

Captain Convery so happened to have a piece of meat that was on the outside of the carcass, and it was just too tough to chew. He did not want to spit it out, so he chewed it as well as he could and then attempted to swallow it. The meat, being hard and dry, and probably too big, stuck in his throat and cut off the air through his wind pipe. He could neither speak nor breathe. He searched out Captain Daily, who was nearby, pointed to his throat and made motions to explain the trouble. Daily opened Convery's mouth, took his own finger and shoved it down Convery's throat as far as he could. The meat went down. If Captain Daily had not been there at that time and if Convery had not been able to find him, Convery would not have finished out the war.

* * *

When the Battalion shipped out from New Jersey, all of the battalion equipment, miscellaneous supplies and luggage had to be marked with a special battalion symbol and marking for each particular unit. When the troop transport ship, a Swedish luxury liner converted to carry 7000 men, arrived at Oran, everything in the hold was dumped onto the landing quay. Consequently, everything from all the units aboard ship was all mixed up and just one great big mess. Captain Daily, while looking for the supplies of the medical detachment, came across a drum of unmarked pure grain alcohol. Knowing that his medical detachment would always have use for the alcohol, the drum immediately became part of his supplies and the future source of his Kickapoo juice.

* * *

After supper one evening, Colonel Bowers, Captain Daily, Warrant Officer Hines, and Captain Convery soaked in some hot baths located in the middle of a desert wheat field. The place was about eight miles from camp. They drove over to it in the ambulance. The plentiful water supply was from a hot spring. It ran through a trough and then through a building with about six rooms. Each room had a large concrete tub, better described as a pool about three feet deep with steps going down from one corner to a larger step, which made it possible to sit down and soak before getting all the way in. The pool was about eight feet across and ten feet long. When they first got in, the water seemed too hot, but after awhile it was like all hot baths and easy to stand. The water came in from one side and flowed out the opposite.

When they arrived, they met several Italian prisoners just

coming out. Italian prisoners were assigned to various farmers and were working as farmhands. The Italians were told about the fall of Catania. They were not a bit concerned. They all wanted the war to be over soon so they could go home. They disliked the Germans and also the French, but they liked the British and the Americans. One of them, through our driver who spoke Italian, said that he had been stationed in Sicily for four years but had never been home, although his home was only 200 miles away.

After the baths, they all had a glass of wine at a wine shop nearby and then went back to camp. The evening's activities helped to provide a good night's sleep.

For one of the dinners, the mess officer had been able to go out and buy some fresh lamb, new potatoes, tomatoes, and onions. They had the roast lamb with potatoes and gravy. Peas and carrots were canned. The fresh potatoes were the first that anyone had had and everyone ate his full share. Going without fresh potatoes really developed a hunger for the tubers. The dehydrated potatoes that were had at that time were nothing like the dehydrated mashed potatoes of today.

The boys built two showers for Battery Headquarters—one for the officers made from a gas drum and one for the enlisted men made from an aluminum wing tank from a wrecked plane. The latter held about 200 gallons. Being flat and of aluminum, the water warmed up nicely in the sun.

August 10, 1943, Captain Convery was made Executive Officer of the Battalion and was back to the point where he was at Camp Hulen where he was Executive Officer of the 457th AA Battalion.

He was proud to be the Exec of what Col. Bowers had been told was the best AA Battalion in North Africa. Another indication of what others thought of the Battalion occurred when several battalions moved from the area. One battalion had to stay behind. The 439th was chosen because the General said that it was the only battalion that could take care of itself without the Brigade's direct supervision.

Convery was Battalion Adjutant before he was made Executive Officer. One of the first jobs he had to do was the signing of the charge sheets for Major Jones's court-martial. Nothing had been heard of the trial and everybody thought that maybe it would be dropped.

An inspection was held by General Tobin which was very complete. He had only complimentary remarks about everything he saw and did not have a single suggestion to make, which was uncommon. In fact, he took back ideas to pass along to other units. He liked the Headquarters Battery area and complimented Sergeant Schrader on it. He was well satisfied with the noon meal that he ate. Things were right and pleased him.

One day during August, four of the officers were gone. That left vacant places at the table. It was suggested to the Colonel that it would be a good night to repay some of the social debts. He promptly invited two British officers, and Convery invited two. Thereupon, Convery checked on what was going to be had for dinner and planned to have the sergeant in charge dress up the mess a bit.

He found that the menu was to consist of plain canned hash and something else that would not have been palatable. He also found that the officers' mess sergeant, as well as the regular table waiter, had gone to a funeral. There he was, guests coming for dinner, nothing to eat, no one to cook anything if he had it, and no one to serve it if it were cooked. The plan had been that they would eat the regular issue meal, which was what was done most of the time, plus a few extras that had been bought from their officers' fund. He believed his neck had been stuck out, and it was sure going to be whacked.

He enlisted the services of Captain Hallberstadt, who sent out a couple of his boys to get chickens from the Arabs. After an hour or so, they came back with chickens, potatoes, and eggs. These were turned over to the kitchen for preparation. They sent into town for onions and tomatoes for salad. The potatoes were fried and served with the chicken, bread (no butter, it had not been tasted since they arrived in Africa), jam, canned spinach, and canned apricots. They managed a very good meal. They called another man to take care of the table, and no one knew there were worries of any kind. A North African cocktail was fixed—Kickapoo juice. It was just about the same as a Tom Collins, without the juniper juice.

All in all, it was a very nice evening and they visited until about 10:00 p.m. Squadron Leader Howard, one of the guests, loved his England; knew all of the English traditions; had a bank position before the war; had his family near London; owned his own home; loved flowers and his garden, poetry, and his pipe. He was a very interesting person.

Later, Convery went to see Howard, and while there he saw a broken folding chair someone had left behind. Being of a backward and shy nature, he asked for it and was very surprised to have it given to him. He brought it back and turned it over to Lieutenant Gober who made a new leg. Then he had a comfortable folding canvas chair which was much better than a straight board to park the bones on.

Also, while there, Squadron Leader Howard told of one of their planes that had crashed taking off. It seems that the plane landed in a field a short distance away and crashed into several Arabs and a mule. Two Arabs were killed and the mule. No one put in any kind of a claim for the Arabs' death, or even reported it, but a claim was put in for the mule for 30,000 francs.

★ ★ ★

Arab and donkey

Another time, an Arab youngster ran in front of one of the Battalion's trucks and was killed. There was quite a bit of work completing reports, obtaining testimonies of the witnesses, drawings of the road, how the truck happened to hit the youngster, etc., etc., and it was all taken in to the French authorities. They looked at it, shrugged their shoulders and said, "Poof. Arabs are a dime a dozen." Their livestock was much more valuable. It caused more trouble to run over one of their dogs than to run over one of them. With narrow roads, a considerable amount of military traffic, many Arabs walking, carts, etc., it was difficult to prevent accidents.

One time one of men from Headquarters Battery was crossing the highway coming back from being on pass. He had ridden about five miles toward camp in one truck and had another mile to go. Another truck came along and, trying to flag down the second truck, he got in the way. The driver tried to swerve to keep from hitting him. In doing so, the truck turned over onto the boy and killed him. The body was taken 84 miles to a morgue and two truckloads of men were sent to the funeral service for him.

There certainly was a lot of red tape, or rather careful paper work, in taking care of a casualty. This, of course, was not a casualty from military action, but the procedure was the same. It was the first.

Sergeant Schrader had an unusual coincidence happen to him. When they were preparing for the service, getting the pallbearers ready, etc., the officer in charge of the morgue and cemetery came over to the chaplain and asked whether the men there would conduct a service for another funeral. It seems a bombardier officer had been brought in, and it was too far away for his outfit to conduct a service. He had been killed in a raid either that day or the day before. The chaplain agreed, of course.

When he received the vital information of the officer, the chaplain was surprised to find out that the officer came from Sergeant Schrader's hometown. He immediately went over to tell Schrader. The officer could not be seen, of course, because the box was sealed shut. It was only through the chaplain's remembering the sergeant's home address that the connection was made. It seems that Sergeant Schrader not only knew and grew up with the officer but had lived in the same block about five houses away; had gone to grade school, high school, and college with him; had fought and played with him. Neither had seen the other since they had gone into different branches of service. As it turned out, Schrader's detail of men conducted the service in North Africa for his boyhood chum from a small town in the Middle West. That was certainly a coincidence that wouldn't happen again except in someone's imagination.

★ ★ ★

Here is a story that was picked up from the British friends. It seems that some clothes were hanging in a closet one morning and were talking over the night before. Said the girdle, "Boy, was I tight last night." The brassiere said, "I was on a bit of a bust, too." From the nightgown came, "I was up all night." And the pajamas said, "I had it easy; it was my night off." Cheerio!

PART II

TUNISIA

September 1943

In the middle of May, the war in Tunisia was over, and the Sicilian campaign had started. Consequently, it soon became time for the Battalion to move forward toward Tunisia. In the first part of September, the Battalion left Setif and headed for an area near Tunisia. As Executive Officer of the Battalion, the Captain had charge of the convoy that traveled the 300-mile trip without any accidents or bothersome incidents .

One interesting event gave the entire Battalion a bit of diversion and relief from the monotony of the trip across the desert lands from Setif, Algeria, to Tunisia. The 120-vehicle convoy passed an Arab home alongside the road. The family's children were all out playing in the bare dirt yard. A young Arab girl of about fourteen stood out in the yard without a stitch of clothing on, waving her torso back and forth, more forth than back. As the trucks full of men passed by, they would whoop and holler for the short time it took to pass.

The convoy arrived at its destination right on time. The place was not nearly as good as the spot they were in the previous two months. It was in a grove of eucalyptus trees that were surrounded by wheat fields, and it was hot. By 9:30 in the morning one would be sticky all over, and not until early the next morning would it cool off. That only left an hour and a half for comfortable sleeping.

It was the responsibility of the Executive Officer to set up camp for Headquarters and to make it as comfortable as possible. It was really important to keep a military unit clean and comfortable because the unit would perform much better than a unit that was not. Several went down the road about six miles and had a shower under a GI shower that was set in the middle of a field near a water point. Just imagine taking a shower in the middle of a wheat field 100 yards from the highway with the moonlight almost as bright as day! Nothing ever felt as good as that shower because up to that time the method of washing off the dust and perspiration was by using a wash rag and a bucket of water. That was not very satisfactory considering that it was done after a period of three days. Every day everyone would be covered with dust so thick that it soaked up the sweat. To keep from standing in mud while washing off, a board or something similar was used to stand on. That was the situation that prompted the development of the expression "Never throw out your dirty water until you get some clean!"

★ ★ ★

The 439th relieved another outfit that had used the same site for about a month. Although they had a good combat record, they were a dirty bunch. The place was alive with flies, caused partly by a dirty kitchen area and poor latrines. They were even using a ditch just outside the grove of trees for their urinal. It was no wonder they had a number of men in the hospital. The 439th was licking the fly problem by keeping the kitchen area picked up and limed, fly-proofing the latrines, etc. Even so, they had several cases of diarrhea.

The grove used for Headquarters was part of a wheat field that belonged to a farmer who had his home located at one end of the grove. One of the men who spoke French learned that at one time the grove had been occupied by German and then Italian troops. The farmer liked the German officers more than the Italian because the Germans seemed a bit more friendlier, even though they didn't treat him any too well.

He had a new Ford V-8 stored in his barn. The German of-ficers confiscated it and drove it down the road a couple miles. Later, all he could find was the license plate. The car had been hit by a shell, killing all of the occupants.

In the sanitizing attempts, the field next to the grove was cleaned up by burning the hay and manure spread around the area. Every so often a cartridge would explode as a result of am-munition previously being dropped in the field. Before starting, they had picked up all that they could find. It was all small bore stuff and did not cause any worry because the cartridges were not in a chamber and there would not be much force to the bullet.

★ ★ ★

The Captain was a guest at an Officers' Club that was really quite interesting. It was built from lumber scraps from packing cases. The roof was made from flattened metal ammunition tins and, of course, was quite low. Screens and mosquito netting were up about four feet from the floor, which permitted a cool breeze to flow through the building located on a knoll. Around the walls and hanging under the ceiling were mats with various colored designs. The floor was of finely-crushed gravel that they had been able to acquire from somewhere. Around the walls were benches and chairs as well as several tables all built from scrap lumber. One table was used for writing and two others were used for stud poker games. The glasses for the bar were the bottoms of wine bottles with the top part cut off. The lights were illuminated by a portable power plant just outside. As it usually happened, the power plant ran out of gasoline. Ash trays were the bottoms of small German bombs filled with sand. Light fixtures had been made from plastic globes hung under the lights and painted blue.

The building was built in an L-shape with the long side about 40 feet long. Across the inside corner was the bar with a rail. The bar was stocked pretty well with bourbon, scotch, brandy, and wine. (No one drank wine unless there was nothing else.) It was pretty hard to get liquor, so no questions were asked. Liquor was not allowed to be taken from the club. A radio went full blast with recordings from BBC (British Broadcasting Co.) beamed to North Africa. The woodwork was painted with a cheap blue and orange water paint that livened up the place. All around the club were pictures of girls that had been cut out and pasted to the woodwork. They had been taken from Esquire. Of course, they were in various poses and attire or, rather, lack of attire, reminding everyone of bathing beauties at home and undoubtedly of delightful moments of days gone by. When the Captain left that little bright spot on the knoll, he followed the road to the highway. In the moonlight the road could only be made out by not being quite as lumpy as when he would stray off. Also it was packed hard from travel. At night no outside lights were allowed. He had the feeling that it was not such a bad war after all.

Once, when at the Officers' Club, Convery was talking to some of the B-26 pilots. It was odd how one branch of the service felt about another branch. He asked a lieutenant from Texas whether they had ever come in contact with any of the transport pilots, hoping that he might be able to locate Bob Swartz of Chehalis, Washington. He drawled back, "Captain, we don't talk or even associate with them fellers." B-26 boys, of course, were flying combat missions all the time and in most respects were up against a much tougher job. He thought that they were a little jealous of the transport flyers because those boys were piling up flying time in their long flights which would undoubtedly help them when it came to getting a flying job after the war was over. He then spoke to a B-26 pilot of the flying fortresses and the reply was, "Humph, anyone can fly one of them four-motored gliders."

★ ★ ★

Battery A had a jackass for a mascot. He was a cute little fellow about two-and-a-half feet high with a head just about as big as he was. He was picked up by some flyers and taken clear to

England by plane for the purpose of either auctioning him off for some benefit or giving him to anyone who wanted him. But, poor fellow, no one wanted him, so he was flown back and given back to the Battery. The Captain's first introduction to him was at one of the gun positions when the jackass came up behind him, stuck his head between the Captain's legs and rubbed his ears. He was coal black and cute as the dickens.

★ ★ ★

On a trip into Tunis, Convery had his ego flattened out. He was walking along on the sidewalk when two good-looking French girls were approaching. About twenty feet away he heard one of them say, "Ooh la la!" The other girl then said, "Oh, Com Ce, Com Ca!" meaning "Oh, So, So!"

Convery and Captain Hallberstadt had gone into Tunis to locate a bootlegger. They found one and bought a bottle of gin and one of whiskey. They had to go down an alley, up some stairs, and down a hall into an anteroom, over which hung a sign, "Detective," to another room. They almost expected someone to look at them through a peep hole and want to be told that "Joe" had sent them (shades of the days of prohibition). They tried out the whiskey. It was the poorest excuse for something to drink that either had ever tasted. It was no doubt made from about one-third grain alcohol, two-thirds water and flavored with burned sugar.

★ ★ ★

A week later, Fred took his laundry to a wash lady and planned on pulling a fasty on the rest of the officers. Ever since they had been able to get their clothes washed, they had never been able to get their cottons starched. They were just washed and ironed. He remembered from somewhere that starch could be made from flour. So, with the aid of his dictionary, he asked the wash lady if she could starch his shirt, knowing that she didn't have any starch. He didn't think there was any in North Africa. She showed him a little bit that she was saving to be used on stiff collars, about enough to fill a quarter-pound jar. She said that she could not use flour but she could use rice. They had quite a time understanding one another but made out okay. In order to show him how she used it, she made motions of putting the rice on a cloth, folding it to make a bag, then squeezing down on the bag like a jelly bag, getting the starch out. The next thing to do was to get some rice.

Fred got some rice from one of the kitchens, took it to the wash lady and had a shirt starched. It came out very well, starched and ironed nicely, but he didn't make himself clear. She starched the shirt, all right, but didn't wash it. The collar was just as dirty as it was when he took it to her. Apparently, she thought he only wanted it starched. The ability to speak French would surely have come in handy.

★ ★ ★

The flies were a real problem. That French farmer's barnyard was right next to the bivouac area. Apparently, a farmer's measure of success was determined by the height of his manure pile. That barnyard certainly did not drive the flies away. The manure pile was the height of the barn and house. The first thing the medical officer did was to go over to the farm and spray the immense manure pile with something that he thought would kill the flies. It kept them back a little bit but not in any noticeable number. An example of the flies' population would be the home of the laundry lady. The kitchen had a single light globe on a light cord that hung from the center of the ceiling. That cord looked absolutely twice its normal size. Actually it was normal size and was covered with so many flies that it looked like a heavily-insulated light cord.

Something had to be done about the flies. Men and officers were carried on stretchers to ambulances for transfer to the hospital because they were so weak from diarrhea that they could not walk. The plan came to build some fly traps similar to small fly traps that had been seen before. Some of the motor pool sergeants were told to see if they could find something in the way of screening from their supply sources. One of them came back with a considerable amount of brass screen that really did the trick.

One of the mechanics made a fly trap from the screen in a circular form about 18 inches high and 10 inches in diameter. The top was covered and inside was a cone of the same material that came up from the bottom, but not to the top, with a small opening at the tip of the cone. There was no bottom to the trap, just the inside of the cone. Around the edge of the round trap were fastened four short legs that held it up about two inches from the ground.

The traps were placed near the kitchen and other strategic points. Underneath they placed a pan with pieces of meat. Sometimes they would put in some wine. Other times water and sugar—anything that would attract flies. The wine was the best bait. When the flies had their fill, they would fly upward onto the side of the cone and then crawl out through the small hole. Then they would be trapped in the compartment outside the cone but inside the larger circular screening. In a day or two the trap would be full of dead flies. The top of the trap would be removed, the dead flies emptied out and the trap would be ready for another batch. If any were alive, they were given a treatment of gasoline.

It was not known the number of cases of diarrhea reported to the medical officer each day at sick call but he said that every day there were fewer and fewer cases reported. Finally, there were very few flies and very few cases of diarrhea.

★ ★ ★

The censoring of letters was done mainly by the officers of the various units. From the officers came stories of men writing home and saying that it was all right for their wives to adopt children—about how the wives wanted to adopt a baby girl or boy. The men appeared dumb for what looked like an excuse to have a youngster running around when they returned home. Or, maybe the men, not being able to do anything about it, just gave their approval in order to make everything appear to be all right.

* * *

Often when Convery went into Tunis to try to do some shopping, every store was closed except the wine shops, barber shops, and the Arab grocery stores. There wouldn't be a store open in which to look around for odds and ends of any kind. The trip was usually a flop. Once, on the way in, he passed some girls trying to hitchhike a ride. One of them had a rather effective way of stopping a truck for a lift. The girls had learned the American method of motioning along the highway with the right hand and thumb to which had been added a bit of France. That is, while the right hand was working with the thumb, the left hand took ahold of the skirt on the left side, raised it waist high, exposing the bare thigh to the hip. It was very effective, because as he was passing and viewing the thigh with amusement, he heard a screeching of brakes. Looking around, he saw the three girls running for a truck that had stopped for them.

* * *

Fred was always looking for something of interest to send home to Esta. He located a rug store and asked about Oriental rugs. He was quite ignorant about them but figured that if there was going to be a time and place to buy an Oriental rug at a bargain that Tunisia was one place to do it. The Arab shopkeeper and his helper spread out a good-looking rug, sat down cross-legged in the middle of the rug and started to bargain. The rug was one that had been woven by an Arabic family. The design and pattern was the same throughout but there were differences as various members of the family had worked on the rug. He thought it would be a good rug to buy. He finally agreed to a price of $20.00 and took the rug back to camp. There he arranged to have it rolled and tied up in a piece of canvas. Before it was tied up, it was spread out on the floor to look at. It was about six feet by ten. Right in the middle of the rug where that shopkeeper had been sitting was a worn spot and hole that he had covered up by sitting on the rug. Fred shipped it home anyway and it became a good conversation piece. He had made a deal and couldn't go back with any degree of success.

★ ★ ★

By September 2, 1943, the British 8th Army had landed at the foot of Italy. Italy had been invaded. All the units in North Africa were being held for deployment in Italy.

★ ★ ★

In October, the 439th officers decided to have a dinner party at one of the hotels in Tunis. The dinner was really good. It was the first time the officers of the Battalion had all been together for a bust since Camp Hulen days. The meal was not much from the standpoint of quantity but was redeemable on the basis of quality. It started out with a slice of melon and a slice of boiled ham as the first course. It was strange but it was good. The next course was soup. After that came the fish course, which was a very delicious white fish of some sort. Then came steak and potatoes. Did that steak taste good! The salad was not too good, based on U.S. standards, but, nevertheless, it was enjoyable because of the oil dressing. Then a dish of French ice cream and, finally, dates were served to munch on. They had French bread with all the courses but without any butter. The local French bread was quite dark but still very tasty. Each course was brought on large platters by waiters, and each plate was served in the dining room from a serving table. They all bought some champagne in addition to the regular wine, and, to top it off, some brandy. The champagne was of 1928 and 1930 vintage, Monopole and Charles Heidrick. The wines had come from France and had been stored away for some time. They were in the private dining room.

If anyone went in for a regular meal, they had no choice and had to take whatever was available. There were always dates for dessert. Dates were used as a dessert everywhere and were always served with a fork. At the officers' dinner they didn't bother to use a fork but instead ate the dates in the normal way with their fingers. Just before they left Tunisia for Italy, they discovered the reason forks were used in eating dates. You were supposed to open them and make sure there were no worms inside!

★ ★ ★

Captain Kimmerer, Captain Daily, Lieutenant Liebe, and Warrant Officer Kaufman went to the same hotel for a regular dinner. Mr. Kaufman was small, heavy set, wore very thick glasses and had a rather round head with rusty hair. Lieutenant Liebe was a very good- looking man. He was about five-feet-ten inches tall, dark curly hair, very dark eyes, and really a very handsome person. As they were leaving the dining room, Lieutenant Liebe spotted a beautiful girl in the lobby of the hotel. Being the Lochinvar type, he decided to make her acquaintance, left the other three, and proceeded on his mission in the true American style. However, before he got to her, she left the lobby and he did not catch up with her until she was outside. When he did, he found out she could not speak English and he could not speak French. However, Kaufman did speak French. Liebe wanted her to go back with him to where Kaufman was in order to have an interpreter and tell her that he wanted to know her. She would not go back into the hotel (probably had heard tales about Americans), so Lieutenant Liebe, by a great deal of motioning with his hands, conveyed the idea that he wanted her to wait where she was while he went after Kaufman. Returning, Kaufman explained to her that Liebe wanted to know her and meet her. Kaufman introduced him and they all started to walk up the street, which happened to be the direction in which she lived. Kaufman carried on a very lively conversation with her, but poor Liebe couldn't understand a word. He would keep asking Kaufman what she was saying, and Kaufman wouldn't answer.

By the time they got to the girl's residence, Liebe was practically frothing at the mouth, while Kaufman was thoroughly enjoying himself, not only to be talking to the girl but also to see Liebe squirm. Finally, when they arrived, Liebe told Kaufman to get the hell out of there because he was taking over from that point on. He was all through with interpreters. Liebe took her up to her doorway, not knowing what to expect. He put his hands on her shoulders and sort of pulled her toward him. She did not object but turned her face and he had to kiss her on the cheek. Then, not being too discouraged, he tried again. This time she turned the other cheek. Liebe thought, "Hell, I guess this is a French custom." Next she took out her handkerchief, carefully wiped off all her lipstick and turned toward him. Liebe told us afterward, "Boys, I'm telling you, I thought I was having a transfusion."

As an anticlimax to the story, Captain Kimmerer and Captain Daily enter the picture. They saw their two friends going up the street with a strange woman, and because the streets were extremely dark (there were no street lights), narrow and winding, they did not know but that Liebe and Kaufman were getting into some sort of trap. They followed along about fifty feet back. Then they caught up with Kaufman and waited for Liebe to join them. It was their idea to protect the other two in the event they were to be held up. What they would have used to stop anyone was questionable because none of them were armed. However, all's well that ends well and all four arrived back in camp okay.

According to Kaufman, Lt. Liebe went back a few nights later. Liebe told Kaufman that he didn't need French anyway, that he could talk better with his hands, said language being good in any country.

★ ★ ★

All of the trucks and jeeps had pet names in addition to their regular numbering systems. Most of the pet names were under the windshields. All of the states were used as well as many of the cities. The majority of the drivers used girls' names, undoubtedly the names of girls at home. Sometimes you saw two or three names, probably indicating interesting conquests. The following were some of the names: Bad Penny, A Little Bitch, Vampire,

Miss Carriage, Who Doo—Who Don't, Baby I Dood It, Earthquaker, Snafu, Vulcan, Mike, Slim, Jeepers Creepers, Homesick, Horsethief, Mudhog and Zeke.

★ ★ ★

The shower was fixed so that they could have a warm (but not hot) shower. To the shower arrangement they had, they added another barrel for hot water which was heated with a desert stove arrangement. A desert stove is a #10 can filled with dirt into which about a half gallon of gasoline is poured and then lit. The gas soaks into the dirt and will burn about an hour. Any other kind of fuel was impossible. Two pipes were run down to a coil made from a shell case to which the pipes were welded. The fire was put under the shell. The heated water circulated up into the barrel. From the barrel, the water ran through a hose to the shower head where it was mixed with cold by a valve arrangement that was acquired from a wrecked house.

★ ★ ★

When Captain Kimmerer was over at the airfield, he arranged for two to have a plane ride in a B25. He invited Convery to go with him. Three crew members took them up—the pilot, copilot, and bombardier. Kimmerer rode along just fine behind the copilot, and Convery rode in the radio compartment with the bombardier who also acted as the radio operator.

They climbed to 8,000 feet. The radio operator asked Convery whether he would like to go back in the tail turret, and of course he said, "Sure." So, the radio operator went forward and told the pilot that he was going back but did not say that Convery was going. After he got behind some clouds and out of sight of the field, the pilot decided to have some fun with the radio operator, so he started in to do evasive action tactics. (They were not supposed to do that when they were just flying for pleasure.) Now, riding in the tail of a bomber at 280 miles an hour (a high speed in 1943) while it was going first up then down then to the left then to the right wasn't the most pleasant of sensations for a plane novice.

They both decided to go forward to the radio compartment and had to walk along on a cat walk between the bomb racks in the bomb compartment. It was quite a sensation to take a step and not be able to put your foot down or, if it was down, not to be able to pick it up. Anyway, by the time Fred got back, his stomach felt a little off. It had the sensation of being full of gas. He thought that maybe if he could burp a little, it would help. He tried but changed his mind in a hurry and swallowed as quickly as possible. Still feeling uncomfortable, he figured the other method of relieving gas might help, but he had to change his mind just as quickly as before. However, everything turned out fine. They landed later with a clean plane, and Convery got out with clean clothing.

The pilots of the airfield being guarded had a friendly feud going on with the pilots of a nearby P-38 field. It seems that some pilots from the P-38 field flew over one day and buzzed the bivouac area in their P-38s (by swooping down low over the ground, friends, and tents). The bomber pilots didn't mind being buzzed, but they didn't like the dust that was raised and blown into their tents. So, to get even, they got into one of their planes and buzzed the P-38 field, flying low over the tents. As they flew over, the pilot dipped one wing in such a way that it clipped along the tops of about 14 tents, knocking them all down. Following that episode, the feud was ended by order of higher authority.

The public restrooms in the North African countries were something else. No one thought very much about it, but the first experience with their unisex restrooms gave everyone a start. Both men and women went into a common outer room that had a row of washbasins along a wall. Over that was a mirror. At either end of the washbasins were doors leading into the room for the *Hommes* and the *Dammes*. The first time Convery went into one there was a nurse standing in front of the mirror combing her hair with her mouth full of hairpins. He wondered if he was in the right place. He said after a couple of times you got used to it, and, as a matter of fact, you had to because there wasn't much else to do.

This story was heard at the airfield: Coming up to Algiers one day a bomber was flying back two Red Cross workers, a man and a woman. When they had been up for some time, the girl said that she had to go to the latrine. Now, a bomber was not built for female travel. It did have a relief tube that the crew used, but for women there just was not anything. The pilot and copilot were gentlemen and felt something had to be done. The plane was searched for a bucket or something, but nothing was to be found. The situation was solved by sending her back into the bomb compartment. The door was closed, and she used the floor of the plane before returning to the area she had been riding in. The copilot opened the bomb bay, which was the floor of the plane when it was closed, and, presto, no problem.

★ ★ ★

Lieutenant Liebe told the story about one day when he was in the restroom of a hotel. While he was standing at the urinal, he was suddenly startled by a feminine voice saying, "Lieutenant, do you have a match?" Needless to say, he was really startled. He reached in his pocket with his free hand but did not have a match. He then had to change hands and reach into his other pocket where he found one and handed it to the young lady. Things like that sure gave you a start.

PART III

ITALY

Naples

November 1943

From the area near Tunis, the Battalion moved to a staging area at Bizerte, Tunisia. All of the trucks were loaded aboard a freighter. Most of the men were put on a second freighter, other than those who had to go along and care for the trucks and guns. They left Tunisia for Naples, Italy, traveled across the Mediterranean, passed Sicily on the west side, and arrived in Naples harbor on 11 November 1943.

The Chief Engineer on the transport ship told a rather interesting story that occurred while the ship was on a trip to Mermax, Russia. The ship was in a convoy and was attacked by a large number of German planes. The ship was loaded with TNT, and any bomb hit would blow it up in one tremendous blast. Four bombs came rather close—just ahead, one astern, one on one side, and one on the other. The mate was on the bridge and somewhat perturbed (who wouldn't be?) and began blowing boat whistles, that is, signals to the other ships. Now, no matter how many whistle signals he blew, none would do any good if a bomb

48

should hit the ship. Someone below said, "Listen to that crazy SOB blowing boat whistles." The mate was kidded about it quite a bit afterward. That was not much of a matter to be kidded about when another ship had just been blown sky high. When the ship returned to the States, every single member of the crew left and absolutely would not be shipped out again.

The Chief Engineer also told about how whenever a convoy got into Mermax the Russians threw a big party for all the crew members and took great delight in drinking as many under the table as they could.

★ ★ ★

Upon arrival at Naples, the ships were anchored outside of the harbor in line with a number of other ships and remained there for several days waiting to be unloaded. One night there was quite a gale. Some of the ships dragged their anchors and drifted together.

The 439th ship had part of its hold full of ammunition. While lying out in the harbor waiting to be unloaded, they had reason to become nervous, as they were there for several days and never knew when there might be an air raid. Because of another stiff gale while moored in the Naples harbor, a ship broke loose from its mooring and drifted into the 439th ship. They couldn't get it away because of the wind, and it was there all night. The lines held, but if they had not, both of the ships would have drifted into another ship which would have piled onto the next ship.

After several days, the ship was moved into the harbor for unloading. The ship with the guns and trucks was tied at a regular dock where its cargo could be handled. The troop ship, with most of the men aboard, was docked alongside an overturned liner that was lying on its side. The hull of the liner was being used as a temporary dock. The engineers had built walks and platforms on the hull. Since the American forces had taken Naples about a week before, the unit was now just a few miles from the front lines, rather than about 300, and moved from Naples to Capua. The Batteries took up defensive positions around a rail head, a supply depot, and a gas dump. It was not until the latter part of January that the Battalion moved out of those positions toward Casino. Everyone hoped to be lucky enough to knock a few enemy planes down and get their Battalion on the scoreboard. Battery B was the first and they claimed a plane.

★ ★ ★

Then came the pay-off. Major Jones was assigned back to the Battalion as he was acquitted at his court-martial. It was not thought that he would make it back, and no one thought Colonel Bowers would permit it without making quite a fuss. What was going to happen now? The Battalion could not have two Executive Officers.

★ ★ ★

Everything in Naples was different than it was in North Africa and also very different than life in the States. The buildings were more or less of the same construction but of a different architecture. A great number of statues and gargoyles, which were not to be seen in North Africa at all, were seen there. The destruction that took place cannot be adequately described nor pictured. It would be just constant repetition describing piles of rubble. Whole buildings of several stories were piles of stones. In other cases, just a corner or maybe a whole side would be gone, exposing all the rooms or just an apartment with its furniture intact, giving the appearance of a huge doll house. It was not anything like Bizerte in Tunisia, which did not have a building left.

As Captain Convery was walking up a street for the first time, a pimp came up to him and wanted to introduce him to his wares. He guaranteed very nice ladies, but the Captain had to disappoint him.

There were a great number of vendors on the sidewalks selling walnuts, peanuts, apples, oranges, and souvenirs—mostly religious pictures inside very cheap and gaudy frames. There were several flower vendors with regular stands such as ones seen in our larger cities. The flowers at that time of year were mostly mums of yellow and orchid.

There were a few dilapidated taxi cabs that looked to have been manufactured about 1935. The drivers were extremely careful in their driving—certainly not the Italian taxi drivers of today. They would almost stop every time they came to a rut in the street. No doubt, they were well aware that when their cab was worn out and refused to run anymore that no new cab would be forthcoming. Convery took a ride in a horse-drawn cart, of which there were many. By doing so, he was able to see a great deal more than he would have by walking or by going at the faster speed of a jeep. The only English those Italians knew was *two dolla'* because that was the price of a 45-minute ride. Later on, when he took another ride which took only 15 minutes, the price was also *two dolla'*.

A great number of people appeared to be living very crudely and entirely within single rooms at the sidewalk level. No doubt the rooms were previously shops or stores. Women were doing their washing on the sidewalks. In a great number of cases there were small fires built on the sidewalks and against the buildings for the purpose of cooking their entire meal in a single pot supported over the fire by bricks. No doubt they had been living in the apartments that had been hit by the bombing.

It was reported that after the landing at Salerno, when the Army started to advance north, it was found that the populace was infested with body lice. In order to protect our own troops, every man, woman, and child was given a treatment of DDT.

★ ★ ★

When Fred was taking his first ride into Naples, he passed what was apparently a municipal building of some sort, because, at the entrance, there were two guards in Italian uniforms and a very fancy dressed policeman—in a blue uniform with red-striped trousers and a long shining saber. To top him off, he wore a cocked hat with white trimming, sitting crosswise on his head. For a minute Convery felt as if he were back about 75 years or else was looking at some Graustarkian movie.

A funeral procession passed with a unique black hearse drawn by black horses which were driven by two coachmen in high silk hats riding on the high seat in front and accompanied by a coachman who rode on a step at the rear. All four sides of the hearse were of plate glass, giving full view of the hardwood and varnished casket which was covered with chrysanthemums. The hearse itself was of highly-varnished, carved wood and very elaborate. Had it been gold in color, the horses white, and the drivers' seat at the base of the coffin, anyone could have convinced him that it was Cinderella's carriage.

Fred had to find a place to get something to eat. A soldier familiar with the area directed him to one that specialized in seafood. After considerable walking and with the help of another soldier who spoke Italian, Fred located the restaurant. The roof was at sidewalk level with steps that went down to the dining area. The restaurant was on the water level with glass across the entire front looking out over the water. It reminded him very much of the restaurant at Rockefeller Center where the restaurant patrons could watch the skaters. In front of the restaurant was a walk, or rather a quay, that had been used at one time to tie up pleasure boats, but of course it then had a very warlike appearance.

The waiters wore white jackets and white ties and did everything very properly, bending at the waist with napkins on their arms and performing in every way experienced and trained waiters should. With their manner of servitude and extreme politeness, Fred had the feeling that they were only interested in what they hoped to obtain from him. His nationality seemed to make no difference whatsoever; they would have behaved the same to a German or a Japanese. There were three musicians playing two violins and a guitar, joined later by a singer. They played a number of songs one never expected to hear, except in the country of their origin—*I'll Be Loving You* and *Down Mexico Way*.

The mixed-fish dinner began with a vegetable soup. Next came the fried fish, which could be recognized as fish and which was very tasty, something like trout. The other pieces of fish didn't taste particularly good. Fred asked the waiter what he was eating (the waiter spoke a little English), and he said that one was mullet and that the other was ink fish or squid.

When Fred found out what he had been trying to eat, he had another drink of wine and tried again, but the wine was not strong enough to overcome the thought of eating devil fish. So, he decided to leave the ink fish to the Italians who had stronger stomachs than he did. For dessert, he had some pastries that tasted good but not rich as pastries go. Needless to say, he left the place, after leaving a tip for the musicians who had been walking around to the tables while they played, still feeling a bit hungry. Walnuts and an apple fixed him up until he got back to a regular GI meal.

The girls were certainly of the opinion that they were there for just one purpose and seemed to have just one idea. Undoubtedly there were a great number of them who were not that way, and probably the ones that the men came in contact with were just the camp followers. Lieutenant Shorthill reported that one mother took her daughter to one of our camps, held the daughter's baby, and took in the cash while the daughter took care of the men. There was a line of 25 men waiting. The Battalion had few venereal disease cases on record. In fact, practically no cases, but in a short time VD cases began to show up.

The civilians seemed to be really short on food and would go to great lengths to get something to eat. The Italian youngsters would hang around the mess lines to get just a bite or two. At one of the camps, a hole had been dug for empty cans and other garbage. On one particular day, one kitchen had corned beef. All of the cans had been thrown into the hole, and before it was covered up, a woman came along with a little girl. She saw the cans in the garbage pit, got down into the hole and scraped the cans, getting a little out of each can until she had about a quart of scrapings. Another time, while the men were in the chow line, a number of youngsters were standing around watching them eat. It is difficult to swallow under such circumstances. One GI had a piece of cheese that he didn't think he was going to eat, so he gave it to one of the youngsters. The GI fully expected him to eat it, but no sir, he put it in his pocket to take along with him, probably to his home.

The attitude of the people in Italy was really quite different from the feeling that was had from the people in North Africa. It was difficult to make them out. They were quite appreciative of everything, but they did not have the look on their faces that the people of Africa did. In Africa it was no trouble at all to get a smile or wave from everyone, but the Italians looked at you with a sort of dumb look, no expression at all.

★ ★ ★

It was quite a job for the Captain to keep his spirits up after Major Jones returned. He really didn't feel like himself. If Jones stayed with the organization, the Captain would be stuck for the duration without a chance of anything better. He was sure that even though Jones was cleared in the court-martial, the facts would be remembered, and it was very unlikely that he (Jones) would ever be given command of the unit should the Colonel be transferred or promoted.

Another thing hanging over Convery was that in a very short while the Battalion was going to be reorganized. The number of officers and men was to be reduced. Officers in the Batteries would stay the same but there would be three fewer in Headquarters. He felt like some sort of a fifth wheel. The Adjutant's position called for a first lieutenant and that was his assignment in spite of the fact that he was Senior Captain in the Battalion. Maybe he would be transferred. The only trouble was that nobody could know where he would be going under the circumstances. It was a tradition that anyone transferred out of the 439th had never failed to benefit from the transfer.

The 457th (Convery's assigned Battalion in the States) wound up in England and, subsequently, became part of the invasion of France and then on into Germany. Captain Herb Jones, of the 457th, his wife Martha, Esta and Fred all had become very good friends. Herb became a major with the 457th and was the Executive Officer. Esta and Martha Jones carried on correspondence over the years. In time, Fred and Esta visited them at their home in North Carolina. When they were visiting Fred and Esta in Washington in 1978, Herb told the story of Colonel Clemmens, Fred's commanding officer at the time his *majority* recommendation was canceled. It seems that Clemmens would not stand up and fight for anything. At one time during some heavy action in France, Clemmens disappeared and was not located until some time later. He had left his unit and gone to hide some distance away. Now Fred knew the reason he had no support from him on that day back in 1942 at Camp Hulen.

* * *

Heavy military traffic made a terrible mess out of the paved roads. The various units would be camped in the open fields with all their vehicles. Whenever there was movement from the camps, all of the trucks and cars would pick up mud from the fields and deposit it on the highways where it became mud soup. Soon the sun would come out, dry up the soup and the traffic would make clouds of dust. All the roads had adjacent ditches at one time, but the continued crowding had converted the ditches to being part of the road.

* * *

In December of 1943 the 439th was able to make themselves quite comfortable in a two-story home that actually had indoor plumbing. It was not as elaborate as some of the buildings being used by various Headquarters, but it was the best thing they could locate around there. They used one large room downstairs for their office and the kitchen. Other rooms were used by various other military sections. The Colonel had his own room and a private bath. Captain Convery had a private room, and the rest of the officers were doubled up. The whole building was heated by individual fireplaces which kept them busy getting fuel as there was not a great deal of wood available.

The building had been hit by shells several times, and because of that they had to make a number of provisions. For example, one of the chimneys had been blown off, and they had to build it up in order to make the fireplace draw. The smoke was driving them out. The water system worked by a hand pump, pumping water up to a reservoir on the roof. Pipes on the roof had been punctured by strafing fire, so they had Lieutenant Gober come up with his motor pool welding outfit and repair the pipes. Because the roof leaked like a sieve, large tarps were fastened down but it still leaked. Quite a bit of the tile on the roof had been blown off but was replaced. To take care of the leaks, #10 cans were used in copious quantities. A power plant was hooked up to the lighting system. So really, what more could they have asked for except their wives.

The house was located on top of a high hill looking out over a valley. Down in the valley was a stream that ran through a grist mill. From this stream the water was pumped up to the roof of the house on top of the hill by an old gasoline engine, which apparently had chugged along in pretty good shape. In order to get the pump to operate (the engine didn't work), a belt was hooked up around one wheel of a jeep and then on around the pulley of the pump. The jeep was started and, presto, water was at the top of the hill.

★ ★ ★

Convery had been able to develop an attitude professing to "not give a damn about how or where the Army pushed him around." He felt he had done a good job with everything. He may not have done it the way with which others would agree, but he had done what he always thought was best. He had also done what he thought should be done and had not limited himself to actions merely to stay out of trouble. All he wanted was for the war to get over and to do what he could to get it over as soon as possible. Whatever he was wanted for or they wanted him to do, he would do. He quit worrying about a promotion. If it ever came along, it would be nice. His plans were definite. He knew what he was going to do.

For several days before the meeting of Roosevelt, Churchill, and Chiang Kai-shek, there were rumors flying around from every direction. Every kind of rumor from A to Z was circulating. Most of them were sure that the war with Germany was about to be over, even down to the day and hour that the order was to be given. There were a number of laughs about the stories and bets being made regarding the end of the war. The rumors never stopped. It was just hopeful thinking by everyone because there was certainly a long way to go.

The roof was fixed by the owner of the building, and from that time on they were not bothered by water running all over. The kitchen of that place was different from anything anyone had ever seen. It was probably the usual kitchen in that part of Italy. The whole kitchen and pantry, which was used for a dining room for the officers, was a blue and white checkered tile for both the walls and floor. The kitchen stove was a good one, located in the middle of the room. The smoke went through a pipe down in the back, under the floor and then up the chimney. It was really quite a convenient arrangement. There was no coil system for hot water but there was a tank on the end with a faucet at the bottom.

* * *

Captain Daily brought back a rather interesting and amusing story. He was talking to a pilot officer of the British Air Force. It seems that one of the officers there mentioned to another in a different branch of the Air Force that he had not been home in over two years. The pilot told the other officer that he was flying up to England in a few days and planned to be there for three or four days before returning. If the officer could get a few days' leave, he could fly to England with his pilot friend and visit his family. It was arranged for the officer to have leave, but he did not have permission to leave the country and did not mention that he might go to England. Without permission he flew home to England and spent the days there with his wife and family.

All went well and the British officer returned to his unit. In two or three months he received a letter from his wife telling him that she was pregnant, which put him in quite a spot. The British Army made allowances for legitimate children but not for illegitimate children. How could he request the allowance? If he reported that he had gone home on his leave, he would be admitting that he had gone AWOL because his leave did not permit him to go to England. If he did not state that he had gone home, he could not admit to being the father of his child, and therefore his wife would become immoral and his own legitimate child would be a bastard. Daily did not know the exact details regarding how things were fixed up, but the officer in question was in quite a quandary for some time. He probably mentioned it to his friends. The story was so good that it spread quite rapidly. His CO, hearing the story and having a sense of humor, realized the situation and changed the orders so that he could have gone to England. Therefore, the child could be born legitimate, and dependency allowances could be claimed.

★ ★ ★

About the middle of December, Fred had the opportunity to go through a real palace in Nancy. It was a very large building built in the shape of a square, surrounding a large main courtyard. There was one part where a wing crossed over. It might best be described as being in the shape of an E with the cross bar toward one end and both ends of the E closed, making two courts, one small and the other large. The sides were over a block long. Most of the building was being used for offices. Rooms in the section that had been used for the royalty were beautiful. The furnishings were all gone, but what was left was definitely worth seeing.

A wide marble stairway of fifty short riser steps was used to get to the second floor. Then the stairs turned back on both sides for another fifty steps. The wide banisters were of marble. At the top of the first flight of steps, there were several large statues. The second-floor landing formed a large rotunda with columns, past which one could look into either of the two courts. The royal wing stretched out from the rotunda. The rooms all had names which couldn't be understood from the Italian guide. The first room had a tremendous gold and brass chandelier hanging from a ceiling of pale blue. All around the cove in the curved area between the ceiling and the wall were white carvings and/or plaster work. The figures were very sharp and intricate, resembling large cameos. At one side stood a large statue of some famous character. The statue had been sandbagged for protection. Most of the bags had been removed except for one double row. The rest of the rooms were finished in different kinds of marble with white woodwork trimmed in gold leaf. Every room was decorated with paintings and murals, not in frames but as part of the walls.

Fresco paintings covered the whole ceiling, some as one large and continuous painting and others as separate paintings with decorative paintings in between scenes. On the ceiling of one room the artist managed to get a three-dimensional effect. It was so distinct that a viewer had to move from one side of the room to the other to see whether a certain figure could cast a shadow or whether he could see behind it. No shadows were cast.

There were historic murals of treaty-signing ceremonies, battles and paintings of famous characters of Italian legend. One room was lined with mirrors extending to the ceiling with large crystal chandeliers that hung at either end. The guide's route went through a dressing room (the bedrooms were closed) and into the bathroom. The bathtub was very deep, very short and of brass. The two faucets looked more like small brass fire hydrants than the usual faucet. The washbasins were of carved marble and looked very heavy. Fred wondered why there were two until the guide said that one was for hot water and one for cold. Of course, there was the ever-present bidet. The living quarters had four bathrooms, each one equipped with a toilet and bidet. A bidet looked somewhat like a toilet, same height, without the seat or cover. It was made of porcelain like a toilet, pear shaped without coming to a point at the front, with the base of the pear rounding out sharply. The inside was flat bottomed and about five inches deep. It had two faucets and a washbasin-type rubber stopper. According to Webster, a bidet is a low, bowl-shaped, bathroom fixture with running water used for bathing the crotch. Fred knew what the bidet was for, but the guide thought he didn't. To indicate what it was, the guide squatted slightly, spread his knees and waved his hand between them. Going back to the royal bathroom, he did not see the toilet, but at one end there was a wooden seat with a hole in it that was identical to any outdoor plumbing installation.

Fred had the opportunity to stand on a balcony on which Mussolini had stood to make his speeches. From the balcony, Fred could look up a long avenue lined with very tall trees. At the end, Mt. Vesuvius was standing with the cloud of smoke that continually came out.

In several of the rooms, the walls were covered with different colored satin surrounding the paintings. Some rooms were pale green and others were pale blue. Throughout there was a great deal of all kinds of marble. There was a large alabaster urn in one room that stood on a pedestal. The urn itself, about four feet high and about three feet across the top, was shaped like a champagne glass. The piece looked like agate-colored marble.

The guide asked a soldier in the group to hold a match inside the urn, which produced a light showing through quite a large area as though there was a strong light inside.

The guide then took them on to other rooms with paintings indicating seasons of the year—a room for each season. Winter was indicated by the characters wearing winter clothing. Flimsy clothing was for spring. The guide's time was up and he had to leave the group. Everyone thought they had their money's worth—25 lira.

At the foot of the hill near where the water was being pumped up to the quarters was an old-time, water-powered, flour mill where the wheat was being ground between mill stones. It was run by an Italian who used to live in New York and was in the American Army during WWI. He had a friend visiting from Scranton, Pennsylvania. Between the two of them, they told some rather interesting stories. The mill had been there for as long as the Italian could remember, and he knew that it had been there as long as his father could remember. The stone being used to grind wheat had been in use for 50 years.

He said that the Germans took all of the produce, ate all of the hens from the area, and there would, therefore, be no eggs until next spring. The cattle had been shipped out leaving the country really bare. He said that they had also taken all of the wheat. They had, in fact, taken everything they could get their hands on. The Italians dug holes in the ground to save some of the wheat and to have some for seed. That explained where the wheat came from that was being ground.

★ ★ ★

The roads were very narrow and winding. Traffic could only go one way. MPs were stationed at intersections to keep the traffic going in the right direction on the right street. The streets were exactly like the alleys of our large cities. The buildings were built right up from the street level with no sidewalks. There was just room for a vehicle and one person on either side. There were doorways in all of the buildings, into homes or stores, but none had steps or porches of any kind. After getting out of the city, the streets were narrower and without buildings. The walls on both sides of the road were made of stone that looked as though they had been there for centuries. All along the wall were marks made by the hubs of two-wheel carts. The indentations gave the appearance of high water or tide marks. The walls must have taken the bumps of thousands of carts to make that long continuous mark. The road was paved with oblong stones measuring approximately one foot by two. Some stones seemed to wear more than others, and some seemed to have sunk down a bit. Many seemed to be mounds. The whole arrangement was very bumpy. When an Army truck passed, the people walking had to flatten themselves against the wall.

Knowing he was going to be released, Captain Convery made a trip to Brigade Headquarters and contacted the AA section people there. He inquired about whether or not they knew of a spot to which he might be assigned when he became released from the 439th. He was told that there was a vacant spot with an Air Force Headquarters that called for an AA officer in charge of the Early Warning System, as it applied to the Anti-Aircraft Artillery. He made a trip to the Headquarters of the Air Force unit and was able to find out that it was possible for him to be assigned there on a temporary basis. Then he went back to Brigade Headquarters and asked for the assignment.

He was put into detached service to the Brigade to take charge of the part of the Early Warning System between the Air Force and the Anti-Aircraft Brigade. He thought that it would be an important assignment. He was glad to get away from the Battalion, even though it was on a temporary basis.

Frattamagoire

━━◆◇◆━━

December 1943

The Captain moved the morning of December 23 and was all settled in the new work by noon. It was certainly a relief to be away from the old setup. He brought along everything he owned and was hoping that he wouldn't have to go back. His new duties could become very important. The work had been getting done, but no one was really taking care of it. He had the feeling that although the Colonel felt that he was putting him in a minor spot, he was actually in a position where an exceptionally good performance would be noticed by people of far higher rank than the Colonel. He also knew that a poor performance would be very noticeable. His work was to be with all of the Anti-Aircraft Artillery in Italy.

The Captain believed he was going to like his new assignment and hoped that nothing would happen to change it. There was nothing permanent about it, but on the other hand, there was nothing permanent about the Army. He was living and messing with an Air Corps group of officers who were friendly and quite congenial. Little things, such as getting a return of *Good Morning* rather than a grunt made a big difference. Also, it was very interesting to be living with officers of the Air Corps Headquarters because there was so much wartime activity they knew about. The mess was very good and the school building that was being used for the officers' quarters was more like a club. They had fixed up a bar and a reading room.

The location of the Headquarters was in a town about seven

miles northwest of Naples called Frattamagoire. It was the Head-quarters of the 64th Fighter Wing. The Wing was in command of all of the fighter planes supporting the 5th Army, later the 7th. The planes were based at various air fields in occupied Italy. A Signal Battalion of about 3,500 men was assigned to the Head-quarters. It was the duty of the Signal Battalion to maintain the communications between the Headquarters, the airfields and all of the radar units located on the high points in the mountains behind the front lines. The radar units were all manned by Signal Battalion personnel of the Signal Battalion.

Radar Unit No 3

Being the AA Officer at the Air Force Headquarters, Convery's duty was to be at the operating room of the Air Force through which all of the radar information came. The radar op-eration at that time was the beginning of radar control of aircraft. The radars furnished bearings or altitudes. By manually plotting the information on the plotting board, the controllers had the information to direct the fighter planes, as well as to keep track of the enemy or hostile planes. The map or board was about 12 feet square with coordinates. The map showed the area covered by the various fighter plane units or squadrons of fighter planes. Above the board and around it was a desk for the controller and his assistants. The controller was the officer who had direct communications with the fighter planes as well as with the fighter plane bases. He would direct the planes in the event there were any hostile planes in the area and provide any other information the pilots should have. There were also other officers who were always in direct contact with the various airfields. The 64th . Fighter Wing was commanded by a General who was in command and who directed all of the activities of the various fighter squadrons in Italy.

Around the board or large map were men who had direct and continuous telephone contact with each radar unit. As the radar units tracked a given plane, the information was passed directly by phone to the individual who would place a marker on the map showing the location of the plane being followed by the radar. By coordinating the information on the board, the controller was able to tell the location of the plane, its altitude (angels— 10 meant 10,000 feet), and the approximate number of enemy planes. The information from each radar was marked on the board with a marker that consisted of a base about two inches in diameter with a post extending up from the center about five inches. On each post was a card giving the flight a number. The number was headed by a letter—such as F, U, or H—meaning friendly, unidentified, or hostile. The marker could be moved by a stick or by hand. As the plot information came in, the markers were left on the board. This developed a track, and the controller could estimate where the flight was heading. The controller, being in contact with a flight leader, could ask his location, and from that and any other information he might have, he could determine whether the flight was friendly or hostile. If he knew neither, he would call the track unidentified until he knew for sure what it was.

★ ★ ★

All of this was the very crude beginning of radar use in warfare. The term *radar* was derived from the phrase "radio detection and ranging." The radar units located at high elevations sent out a continuous beam of electromagnetic waves that would reflect back to the radar units. This would indicate the presence and range of objects in space and their direction.

It was the duty of the AA Officer in the Control Room to see that the information about any hostile planes showing up on the board was passed to Brigade Headquarters. Brigade then passed the information to the various Anti-Aircraft Artillery units. Convery was the only AA Officer.

Convery, as an AA Officer, really ran into a hornets' nest when he began living and associating with the Fighter Wing Headquarters officers. Practically all of the officers were ex-fighter pilots who had completed their required number of missions and were assigned to various units. In the past, sometimes our own AA would fire on our own planes. This was because our AA gunners did not know whether the planes were hostile or friendly and visual identification was extremely difficult. No AA gunner wanted to wait until a bomb was dropped or he was strafed before he determined whether a plane was friendly or hostile. The gunners would take a chance and fire. In other words, "Shoot first and ask questions afterwards." When this happened and the planes were fired upon, the pilots would believe they had been flying over hostile AA, and they, in turn, would come back and bomb or strafe the positions.

In the landing at Salerno, the Fighter Wing was right in the middle of it. (Salerno, about thirty miles south of Naples, was the site of the U.S. landing in Italy.) It seemed that there was quite a bit of aircraft support for the landing. An unknown gunner had a nervous finger and fired on some of our friendly planes. As soon as this took place, all of the other gunners thought the planes were hostile and began firing. The guns on the naval ships responded and started firing. As a consequence, a number of our own planes were shot down by our own gunners. This created a terrific animosity in the fighter pilots toward AA Artillery.

When Convery walked into the building where he was to be billeted and met some of the officers, they already knew he was an Anti-Aircraft officer, and the reception was really cool. When he was introduced to one of the Air Force officers, the remark was made, "Humph, one of them guys, eh?" There was no question how he and the others felt. The atmosphere remained cool for quite some time.

★ ★ ★

From the Control Room the controller or one of his other officers assisting him had radio contact with the fighter pilots and had been told a number of times that they were being fired upon by our own AA artillery when the planes were over the front lines. Convery went to General Barcus, who was in command of all of the fighter planes, and told him the stories some of the pilots had been bringing back. He also went to Brigade Headquarters and talked to them about the situation. His next move was to go to General Barcus and have him send out a directive to all of the airfields and to the pilots that, in the event that they were fired upon by our own Anti-Aircraft artillery, they were to make a report, furnishing the exact location, time, date, and consequences. Then, he went to Brigade Headquarters and had the Brigade send the same order to all of the Batteries of AA Artillery. That is, in the event that any AA emplacement suffered any bombing, strafing, or any hostile activity from any friendly aircraft, they were to make an exact report of the date and time as well as a description of the plane, with any identifying numbers. Believe it or not, no reports were filed by either the anti-aircraft or the fighter planes, and it was not long before the criticism began fading away.

★ ★ ★

The building in which Convery was billeted was a former

schoolhouse. He had a cot in one of the schoolrooms. On January 3 he was moved about two blocks away to a room which had been part of an apartment. It was much better. The Operations Room was kept going 24 hours a day. Consequently, there had to be an officer on duty passing on information to Brigade Headquarters at all times. He had Brigade assign four officers to work with him who were all AA lieutenants.

★ ★ ★

The harbor of Nancy had an air raid. It was really quite a sight. All around the harbor tracer shells were being fired on the raiding planes. Convery was watching from a point outside the school building. When it was about over, one of the German planes flew over very, very low—keeping under the radar coverage. Two and a half years later, while on his way home, there was a German prisoner assigned to clean the showers. Coincidentally, he turned out to be a German pilot who had been on that raid to Naples and had left the area flying as low as he could. Maybe he was the one Convery saw.

★ ★ ★

Some of the Italians at that time were unusual people, doing many things in a crude way. For example, for two weeks they worked on a dirt street two blocks long and still did not have it completed. Army trucks were furnished to haul the crushed rock for the base and fine crushed rock for the surface. The trucks were unloaded with hand shovels, but instead of moving the truck and unloading the gravel in several small piles, they unloaded it all onto one pile and then spread the rock. They shoveled it into baskets and carried the baskets on their shoulders to where they wanted it. It certainly was a waste of time.

★ ★ ★

Fred's room was part of an apartment owned by a Signor Funnari. There were three girls and a young man in the family, and Fred became friendly with all of them. He was playing quite a bit of bridge. Captain Butler, Lieutenant Wilke and Fred often went to Fred's room and played bridge with Signor Funnari. It was fun playing bridge in Italian. Signor Funnari was a good bridge player and enjoyed it. They would play until after 11:00 when Convery would go on duty at midnight.

★ ★ ★

In the middle of January, the weather began to turn warmer, and at times it was quite pleasant. Other times it was really cold, and it was difficult to understand how some of the people lived in that weather. Either they did not have warm clothing at all or had lost it during the fighting in that area. Youngsters as young as two years, barefooted and bare bottomed, would be on the sidewalks, while GIs, fully dressed, would be wearing extra clothing. On the warmer days, the women would all come out onto the sidewalks in front of their buildings to nurse their babies. If we had not had air superiority, no one would have been on the streets.

★ ★ ★

One evening Fred was invited to have dinner with the Funnaris. The night before, Signor Funnari asked whether Fred liked meat or fish better. Meat was hard for them to get, so he said fish. The dinner was good but somewhat strange. A large dish of homemade macaroni, seashell style, was the first course. Then, fried fish, which was mullet and a little squid. It was not too hard to eat. Apparently, Fred was getting used to Italian ways. The next course was cold cauliflower and olives over which was put olive oil and vinegar, and that became the salad. He was surprised to find it tasted very good. Red wine was served. The family consisted of Signor and Signora Funnari; their son Santino, age 23; their oldest daughter Angela, age 22; another daughter; and Mina, the youngest, age 10.

★ ★ ★

Frattamagoire had a rope factory that had been shut down and was not operating. The factory employees were making rope by hand. At various homes people were doing what might be called *carding the hemp*. They whipped it and drew it through pegs protruding from a log and worked it into skeins. Then it was twisted into strands. One person twisted the strand by using a wheel arrangement; the other walked backward until he had a strand about 50 feet long. Then, those strands were twisted together to make a rope.

★ ★ ★

Angela Funnari said that Santino, her brother, had to be hid during the German occupation. To do this they dug a chamber in the ground and kept him in there all the time. They dropped food to him through a hole. He never left the chamber. She did not say how long he was there, but it must have been quite an ordeal. Santino had to be hid from the Germans to keep him from being forced into the German Army.

Both Santino and Angela could speak very good English. While visiting with Santino, he asked what the words *war bonds* meant. He had seen it on matchbooks and in some other places. It was quite a job to explain. He then asked what *out of bounds* meant. He had the two tied together. The explanation was that *out of bounds* was British for *off limits*.

★ ★ ★

In Africa, the French picked up our phrase "OK." Whenever a Frenchman started rattling off in French, and now the Italians in Italian, the usual American soldier would say OK. So, OK became a byword. Angela asked what it meant because all of her friends were saying it. One asked her to ask what "*It beats the hell out of me*" meant. Someone had been having fun. Most of the kids said, "*OK, Joe.*"

In Africa all of the kids would ask for *bon bon*. In Italy they all wanted carameli. One little shaver about five years old was taught to say "Thank you" by a GI. As the GI was going to supper, the little fellow spotted him about a block away. He started running toward him, "Hey, Americo, thank you, carameli." The combination of what he was yelling, his running, and a wide dirty grin was hard to resist, so the shaver got a little extra. Hard candies were part of the rations and were always included in with the "C" rations.

The Funnaris were very nice. Every once in awhile they would send in coffee to Fred in the mornings if he was in his room, or tea in the afternoon. They brought some tea one time, and he gave them some of the bags Esta had sent. After that, the servants brought in tea regularly, always on a tray and in a small silver pot that only held one cup, with several slices of lemon that had been peeled before being cut.

While visiting with Santino, he said that the women who went with men without a third person accompanying them were the wicked women.

Captain Butler, the Adjutant, said that Major Selby, the Senior Controller, was bucking hard for the assignment of AA Officer on the Fighter Wing Staff. The TO (Table of Organization) called for a lieutenant colonel in that particular spot, and Major Selby would like to have it. However, Major Selby was an Air Force officer.

In keeping communications open, the Signal Battalion would take telephone lines that had been damaged by the fighting and put them back into shape, making whatever use they could of them. There were a great number of telephone linemen in the Battalion.

Captain Convery would make trips out to the various AA Battalion Headquarters as well as to Brigade Headquarters and advise them of the information available and try to get them the Early Warning of approaching hostile planes. Nothing in that respect had been done in the past.

It was the responsibility of all units to run their telephone lines upward to each one's command. That is, a Company or Battery ran its telephone lines to the Battalion Headquarters, Battalion to Regiment, Regiment to Brigade, etc. The Air Corps would make the information available at certain points, and from that point on, it was the responsibility of the AA .

Early Warning was vital to an AA unit. The guns were all manned by a crew, but obviously no crew could stay on duty at a gun site 24 hours a day. It was not necessary because planes were not in the air all of the time. So, any Warning they might have had, whether a minute or five minutes, was invaluable. The heavy guns were for the high flying planes, and the 40 mms were for the low flying. Without Early Warning, the guns were dependent on their own observations, which was the trouble they had regarding firing on friendly planes. It was very difficult to tell whether a plane was hostile or friendly. The plane speeds were increasing with every new model to the point that in 1944 the gun crews hardly had time to sight an enemy plane and start firing before it would be going out of range.

The control board was the best source of information for determining whether planes in the air were hostile, friendly, or unidentified. The board with its various plots would develop a track showing the point from which the plane has been coming and indicate where it was going. If there was a hostile plane, or planes, on the board, the controller notified our fighter planes in the air and let them know the approximate location. The AA Officer on duty passed the same information to the guns on the Early Warning system. If the radars indicated a flight of enemy planes headed our way, the controller or one of his assistants would call a fighter squadron and tell them to scramble, and they would take off to meet the incoming hostile flight. The AA Officer would alert the Anti-Aircraft Artillery giving the gun crews time to get ready to start firing when the enemy planes came within range. However, the system was only as good as its communications.

Controllers looking down on control board

It should be mentioned here that the radars of 1941, 1942, 1943 and 1944 were really in their infancy. Later developments made terrific improvements. Nevertheless, those first radars did an excellent job. Improvements were continuous and kept on developing right up to the current times with radars installed on jet liners that can see to the horizon. In an attempt to have some Early Warning of a plane, a sound system of ears was developed in the late 1930s. That program did not work because of the increasing speeds of the airplanes which were beginning to fly at speeds approaching the speed of sound. Consequently, the target would come within range of the guns at about the same moment as the Early Warning sound reached the guns. Another source of warning and assistance to the Anti-Aircraft guns were the searchlights. The lights helped to locate the planes at night making raids on harbors and other installations but were not effective during cloudy weather, nor could they do anything about a warning that the planes were coming. The radar was the real and only answer to the necessary Early Warning to the Anti-Aircraft Artillery.

Control board

When playing poker one night, a British squadron leader joined the game. He had a little too much to drink. All of the chips were worth 25 cents—red, white, or blue. He could not quite get the money value right. It was explained to him that the red chips were 25 cents, the blue chips, two-bits, and the white a quarter. There was a lot of fun at his expense. It was a job to keep the money and the values straight. There were francs, lire, shillings, pence, and, of course, dollars and cents, as well as pounds. It was difficult to be sure of one's self when it came to British monies.

Invasion at Anzio

January 22, 1944

This was the day the American forces landed at Anzio. The following is an excerpt from a diary written by one of the men in the Advance Operations Room at Anzio:

It is now two a.m. Capt. E. Jordan, our Senior Controller, and two men have set up an F/M on the ship's top deck. The show starts on time and there is no noise but the steady rumble and flash of our naval bombardment. Our radio nets keep careful check, and about five in the morning we get reports that all of the landings have been successful. The operations are going forward as arranged. The first eight waves have reached shore and now they are beginning to meet a little enemy opposition.

The Rangers have taken both Nettuno and Anzio in twenty minutes! They have taken the Germans by complete surprise. When dawn comes we are about two miles off-shore with nothing but our own ships as far as we can see. This was not to last very long. Pretty soon an enemy air raid came down on us. All hell broke loose. JU-88's dropped their bombs on the boats and close to shore. The anti-aircraft gun crews are alert as can be and really give the Jerry a lot of hell. They got about five out of twelve.

We proceeded to move into the beach, and a minesweeper beside us hit a mine and went down in seven minutes; seven men were saved. That is a great loss, but on we all go and presently there comes another raid. All hell broke loose again and they dropped bombs around the boats. All were scared as hell and the feeling of helplessness was a great strain. We soon hit the beach and we were never so glad to hit old Terra Firma as we were at the moment. The unloading took most of the day and the men would snatch a can of C-rations when they were just too weak from hunger. Most of our trucks had to stay close to the beach. It was getting dark and we tried to go to sleep around the trucks.

As soon as it got dark, Jerry started laying them in. That German 88 is the wickedest gun that ever was. It was a heavy barrage and they kept it up most of the night. The morale was good and everybody was trying to make the best of a bad situation.

★ ★ ★

26 January 1944

The weather is bad and there is very little air activity. The men are very nervous, but, nevertheless, the operations are going on fine. 1900—a heavy raid is on at this moment. Flares are reported all above the docks at Anzio. We can feel the bombs and hear them through our ack-ack. They have hit one of our ammo dumps and it is going into the air. Our ack-ack has shot down five Jerry bombers, and one of our night fighters reported shooting down a Heinkel. The strain of these raids and of the incessant shelling is telling on the men, and they are all on edge; nevertheless, everyone is sticking to his post and doing a wonderful job in the operations.

For a few days the Ops block continued to operate in the woods of the Villa Borghesi, but when close hits from 88s blasted out the windows and filled the sides of the vans with shrapnel, it was time to move. The first shift was made to a railroad tunnel on the estate. The Army requisitioned this location for ammunition storage purposes; so the Ops block and a small filter room were moved to a tunnel used as a Headquarters by Lt. Gen. Mark Clark, commanding the Fifth Army. A substantial earthen roof that could have withstood anything but a direct bomb hit protected "Grubstake." At the tunnel openings sandbags were piled to withstand concussion from the near misses.

Lt. Lonnie Temple, who was formerly with the telephone company before coming into the Army, was in charge of all telephone wiring construction and other communications. He was in charge of the rewiring of phone lines on poles that had been damaged during the fighting. He told a story about a radar unit that was starting to use some of the lines that had been put back into service. An operator picked up a phone and plugged into the switchboard. At the other end of the line was some German conversation. He listened for quite awhile, but not being able to understand it, he knew nothing. Apparently, the German heard some of the American conversation and the line was cut.

It was always a big question as to how the people managed to exist. They appeared to eat only bread and vegetables. The vegetable was only spinach greens. They cooked large pots of greens on the sidewalks, poured the water into the gutter and ate the greens. That was their meal. They mixed their flour into dough for bread and carried that to the bakery. The loaves were round, about 12 inches in diameter, and carried on large, four-foot-square, flat boards on their heads. It was always a temptation to tip one of them over. The community bakery used an old-fashioned brick oven.

★ ★ ★

In talking with Major Schier at Brigade Headquarters, Captain Convery was told that there was now good and effective liaison between the Air Corps and the Ack-Ack, the slang term for Anti-Aircraft or AA Artillery. To anyone who is unfamiliar with the term *liaison*, the definition is "In military use, inter-communication between units acting as neighbors or in conjunction."

★ ★ ★

January of '44 turned real cold and it was difficult to find any place to keep warm. There was no heat in any of the rooms at the Funnaris. They kept warm in the evenings by sitting around a brass brazier that burned charcoal. A brazier was about two feet in diameter and was like a large saucer on three legs. Every once in awhile someone would stir up the coals to make the coals burn a little harder and throw out a bit more heat.

★ ★ ★

In the early part of February, an organization was formed of Austrian and Polish soldiers who had been forced into the German Army. They had escaped from the German Army and had come into allied territory offering their services. The Army Air Force took German aircraft that had been shot down, removed the radios, with their crystals, and set up a station to monitor German aircraft with the Austrian and Polish soldiers. They then could listen to not only all German aircraft transmissions but anything received from other German Army Headquarters. Those men spoke fluent German and, of course, were familiar with all German slang. Their location was top secret. Lines were run to their unit, connecting it to the Operations Control Room. The information they received by monitoring the radio transmissions of the Germans was sent to whatever Headquarters would benefit by it.

★ ★ ★

The unit code name, "Peeper", was used by our Control Room. Very often, the controller, in watching an unidentified flight on the board, would have no idea whether the flight was friendly or hostile. He would call Peeper on the line and ask them whether they had anything coming from that particular area. Peeper had direction finders to use along with their other equipment so that if they had a transmission that they were monitoring, they could tell where it was coming from. They could very often identify the plane or planes as being German, and the controller in the Control Room would label that plot on the operations board as being hostile. At that point, everybody would be alerted, and if we had any fighter planes in that area, they would . be sent to that point to attempt an encounter. At other times, planes would be ordered from their airfields. The AA officer on duty would then pass the information over his line. He would give a continuous report regarding the plot's coordinates and all the AA would make their own tracks, alert their guns, and start searching for the planes. Having that excellent Early Warning made it possible for the crews to get on their guns and be ready for the planes when they came within range in their sector.

One day, Peeper contacted the controller and said they were getting a reception apparently from two German planes and that they were able to give the approximate location. The controller contacted radars in the area and they started tracking the German planes. The controller contacted two of our fighter planes flying near that sector and gave them the location of the two German planes. The American planes were being plotted on the board and everybody could all look down onto the board and see the plots of both flights. Soon the Americans transmitted back to the controller that they were in the area and had spotted the German planes from a point considerably above the Germans. The American pilots told the controller that they were going to attack the German planes. Soon Peeper came on the line and said they were monitoring the conversation between the two Germans and that the Germans had spotted the American planes. So, for a while the controllers had the conversation going, or rather had the information coming, regarding what our planes were doing.

And Peeper was giving the information from the Germans about how they perceived the situation and what they were doing about it. It really was quite exciting. Eventually the Americans were able to report that they had shot down the two German planes. Peeper reported that one of the Germans transmitted that he had been hit and was going down, and, of course, there were no more transmissions from the second plane, just the report from the American pilots.

★ ★ ★

French military units were available to the Allied Forces, but with France being occupied by Germany, they were without Army supplies or equipment. Consequently, they were supplied with everything needed from U.S. depots. Our troops would see the new uniforms, equipment, etc., being used by the French and really gripe and complain. Captain Convery felt the same way until one day when he was going through a valley near Anzio that had just been taken the day before. He changed his mind about the French using our supplies when he saw dead Frenchmen in U.S. uniforms and knew that it could have been U.S. troops in that clothing.

Newspaper clipping from the *Stars & Stripes Weekly*, Anzio Beachhead, Italy:

Second Lieutenant Leroy B. Woodley of 2125 E. Hillyard Road, Richmond, Virginia, an artillery observer attached to a specially trained U.S. force, was standing on a chair on the top floor of an Italian farmhouse peering through the window. Lieutenant Woodley was directing fire on a company of Germans who were attacking across the large canal which runs along the force's sector on the Fifth 's Anzio-Nettsuno beachhead.

The slim lieutenant is an inveterate gum chewer, and as he peered through the dusty panes at the advancing enemy, his jaws worked with increasing rapidity.

"Adjust with impact and fire for effect with time," he shouted over his shoulder to the radio operator who relayed the information back to the Batteries.

A moment later the reply came back, "On the way." Lieutenant Woodley paused expectantly in his gum chewing to watch for the bursting shells. A few seconds later great mushrooms of black smoke sprang from the ground a little to the right and behind the Germans. "Too far," muttered the lieutenant to himself. Again he resumed his gum chewing and shouted over his shoulder, "Two hundred left—one hundred short."

This time the bursts landed in the designated area. The Germans hit the ground when they heard the shells come screaming in. A lot of them didn't get up after that.

When the smoke cleared, there was little evidence of activity out front where the enemy had tried to cross the canal. Gray-clad forms lay inertly in little bunches about the field, now pockmarked with shell craters.

A few of the Germans who were fortunate enough to be able to run were scurrying back from where they had come. Lieutenant Woodley smiled slightly and stroked with his fingers his lean unshaven chin. "I think that ought to hold 'em for a while," he said to the radio operator. Brief Pleasure.

Artillery observer Woodley's satisfaction was momentary, however, for at that instant a squad of Germans was on the point of entering the ground floor below him. In his interest in the Germans to his front, he had neglected to notice what was occurring under his very nose. As he casually lit a cigarette in anticipation of a few moments of peace, his eye chanced to drop to the yard below. The cigarette fell to the floor; the lieutenant's mouth dropped open in surprise. He jumped down from the chair set before the window and bounded over to the radio, "Three hundred short," he yelled into the transmitter, "And fire like hell—the Jerries are coming!" Then he and the operator raced to a window in the rear of the house and jumped out.

Two stories is quite a drop, but the situation was not one to permit squeamishness, and Lt. Leroy B. Woodley was in no frame of mind to hesitate. He and the radio operator both accomplished the jump without injury. Lieutenant Woodley grinned and shoved another stick of gum into his already overworked jaws, "I guess I must have looked like Superman as I came hurtling out of that second story window—but then what else could I do?" From his new observation post the artillery officer watched his shells as they dropped around and on the house which only a few minutes before he had vacated. "I think, all told, that we accounted for at least a hundred Jerries," said Lt. Woodley.—D.H.W.

★ ★ ★

A strange thing happened at one dinner with the Funnaris. A girlfriend of Angelina's was there, and it turned out that her father owned the house that the 439th was in before they moved north. It was their summer home. She and her family were there just before the Germans left that part of the country. She said that her father had hidden a box of money under the floor in the kitchen, but when her father returned afterward, someone had dug it up. Also they left quite a bit of bedding. When they returned, it was all gone. The mattresses, etc. had been used in the trenches around the house. When the house was hit, the Germans moved to another one nearby and then to an air-raid shelter. Of all the people, it was certainly odd that Fred should meet her. She was about Angelina's age or younger. She said that before the 439th left, her whole family had gone up there and had dinner with Colonel Bowers.

★ ★ ★

In war-torn Italy the civilians had to learn how to live without many conveniences. One was power and lights. Fred's quarters had no lights. The Funnari apartment was only about two blocks away from Headquarters and the Ops Room. Lt. Temple had his crew run a power line from Headquarters to his room, and he had the luxury of lights. Without saying anything to him, Signor Funnari thought that he could connect his lights to the power line in Fred's room and have some lights also. It was not long before he was told to tell Signor Funnari that the power plants could not furnish power to civilians.

★ ★ ★

The Funnaris wanted to do something nice for Fred, so because he had to go a long ways to get a shower, they offered him a hot bath. The family all entered into the event. Carmella who worked for the Funnaris got the water hot. Margareta offered him a towel. Maria helped with the water. He had been told about the bath the day before and Angelina told him again. Signor Funnari took him into the bathroom and locked the door. After the bath was over, Carmella had to dip the water out of the tub and pour it down the toilet because the drain was plugged.

★ ★ ★

Occasionally, rations included butter and it sure tasted good. Eggs were all local, of course, and were about 25 to 35 cents apiece, so they were not had very often. Near the officers' mess was an Italian dairy where Fred would have liked to go and get some milk but was a little afraid of it. Every morning the people around there went for their milk and came back with all shapes of bottles. Some appeared to be holding as little as a fourth of a pint. Nearly all of the bottles were wine bottles. He never did see a milk bottle. An Italian breakfast was supposed to consist of milk and some bread, never coffee.

★ ★ ★

There was a rest camp on the Isle of Capri, and because most of the Wing officers had been there, the General of the Wing let the Captain's section use part of the allotment. One of his officers went there for three days. The rest of his group had to take up the absent officer's time in the Operations Room. Fred let the other officers go first and then he went for his R & R (Rest & Recreation).

An old man who acted as an interpreter for the officers of the Wing Headquarters got himself in the dog house once and just sat around all day feeling sorry for himself. Several times he was taken along for assistance in buying things that were needed. They discovered that he was telling them prices that were more than those being asked. He was making a deal with the store-keeper and keeping the difference for himself. Then he would want additional pay for his services. No longer was he needed. He was just another Italian who went to America, made some money and then returned to Italy, never appreciating America enough to become a citizen. He was in America 35 years and one time played in Paul Whiteman's orchestra.

There were a lot of grapes grown around Naples, and in that particular locale they were grown quite differently. They had elm trees planted in rows about 50 feet apart. The trees were topped and trimmed so that only a few branches were growing near the top, which was about 30 feet high. The grapevines grew up the trunk of the trees and were trained to go over to the next tree on wires. There were about six or eight wires going between the trees. A barked branch was put up between the trees for additional support when the wires were loaded with grapes. Barked trunks of smaller trees were used to make ladders to lean up against the wires and vines during the harvest.

There were two towns next to one another, both beginning

with "Fratta." One was larger than the other, so they were named Frattamagoire and Frattaminori, Bigfratta and Littlefratta.

★ ★ ★

People around Frattamagoire who could not afford shoes wore a form of wooden shoes. The shoes were really not shoes at all, just pieces of wood like the sole and heel of a shoe and about an inch thick. A strip of heavy cloth was nailed across the toes. The arrangement worked like a slipper. The heel part dropped off at every step. To keep the shoes on, the women sort of shuffled along, making a clacking noise. The men did not wear them. The better classes had shoes.

★ ★ ★

Frattamagoire appeared to be a very poor section and it was filthy. The streets were swept continually by street sweepers, but even so, the streets were dirty. The sweepers used a broom which looked like the kind used by Halloween witches. The brooms were made of branches of trees tied to a stick, with the sweepers using a sideways swinging motion. There were a great number of horses, which, of course, was the reason for the street sweepers. In addition to the horses, the people made quite a mess. They threw out their orange peelings, ashes, and everything else. Adults were not seen leaving their stools on the dirt sidewalks but there were any number of youngsters. From the visible, sizable evidence, the adults must have come out at night. Afterward, they sometimes covered it over with ashes and swept it into the street, which, of course, made more work for the street sweepers. The sweepings were hauled away in carts to fertilize the fields. That was the reason it was forbidden to eat any fresh vegetables.

★ ★ ★

The medical officers had duties other than office calls and the treatment of colds, illness, etc. The biggest problem of the medical officers was to keep the military personnel in good health and useful to the Army, Air Force, or whatever. A sick soldier was absolutely worthless. A lot of money was spent on his training, and that training was wasted if he was unable to perform his duties because of illness. Furthermore, he had to be taken care of. Consequently, the medical officers did everything in their power to keep everyone healthy at all times and to avoid anything that might cause an illness. The foregoing illustrates one of the problems. Certainly a situation like that would create many illnesses. The medical officer of the command went to the mayor of Frattamagoire and told him that it was forbidden for any of the people in Frattamagoire to use the streets for their toilets. If they continued to do so, they would be required to vacate the area and move elsewhere. That seemed to stop the practice, and the streets became cleaner.

There were quite a number of incidences of venereal disease, as mentioned before. The medical detachment launched a campaign to do everything it could to stop the spread of the disease. Whenever the MPs saw any girls on the streets who appeared to be soliciting, they were picked up, taken to a medical center and given tests to determine whether they were diseased. Many of the girls picked up were highly insulted and naturally so. However, the number of infected cases discovered seemed to justify the action.

Another program that the medics used was adopted from the Burma Shave advertising program of the 1930s. The Burma Shave people made signs about ten inches by thirty-six, fastened them on stakes about five feet high and placed a series of them along the roads and highways about one hundred feet apart. The idea was that the motorist would read the signs as he drove along the road. That was before our present-day system of freeways. Each board or sign would have a few words of a jingle. At the end of the jingle would be BURMA SHAVE. The signs were painted red with white lettering.

The Medics used the Burma Shave program to educate the military. "Take a Pro," was slang for "Take a Prophylactic." Some of the jingles that the medics used were ones like these:

Girls Who Take in Borders—
Give Social Disorders—
TAKE A PRO

•

Mail From Home —Builds Morale—
Don't Let it be Spoiled—By a Dirty Gal—
TAKE A PRO

•

Though Your Girl—May Look Like Venus—
She Still Can—Infect Your Penis—
TAKE A PRO

★ ★ ★

Newspaper clipping from *Stars & Stripes Weekly*, "The Roving Reporter" by Ernie Pyle, February 21, 1944:

IN ITALY—Most infantry companies in the American front lines are now composed largely of replacements, as they are in all armies after more than a year of fighting.

The new boys are afraid, of course, and very eager to hear and to learn, and they hang onto the words of the old-timers. I suppose the anticipation during the last few days before your first battle is one of the worst ordeals of a lifetime. Now and then one will crack up before he has ever gone into action at all.

One day I was wandering through our olive grove, talking with these newer kids, when I saw a soldier sitting on the edge of his foxhole wearing a black silk opera hat. That's what I said—a tall, black, opera hat. At first I couldn't believe it, but it was true.

The owner was Pvt. Gordon T. Winter. He's a Canadian who happened to be in the States on draft registration day, so he registered and then went and enlisted. His father owns an immense sheep ranch near Lindbergh, Alberta, 200 miles northeast of Edmonton.

Pvt. Winter said he found the top-hat in a demolished house in a nearby village and just thought he'd bring it along. He said, "I'm going to wear it in the next attack. The Germans will think I'm crazy, and they're afraid of crazy people."

In the same foxhole was a thin, friendly boy who seemed hardly old enough to be in high school. There was just fuzz instead of whiskers on his face, and he had that eager-to-be-nice attitude that spelled him as not long away from home.

He was Pvt. Robert Lee Whichard of 3422 Leverton Avenue, Baltimore. It turned out that he was only 18 years old. He has been overseas only since early winter. He has seen action already. He was laughing and telling me about the first time he was in battle. Apparently, it was a pretty wild melee and ground was changing hands back and forth. Pvt. Whichard said he was lying on the ground shooting, or maybe not shooting, I don't know, because he admits he was pretty scared.

He happened to look up and here were German soldiers walking past him. Bob says he was so scared he just rolled over and acted like he was dead. Pretty soon mortars began dropping and the Germans decided to retire, so they came back past him and he still lay there playing dead until finally they were gone and he was safe.

Another soldier came past and said he dreamed the night before that he was home and his mother was cooking pork chops by the tubfull for him to eat. This one was Cpl. Camal Meena, whose father is a Syrian minister in Cleveland, Ohio.

The post office system has broken down as far as Cpl. Meena is concerned. He has been overseas five months and never yet got a letter. The corporal has not been in combat yet, but is ready for it. He says he hasn't decided whether he's going to be a minister like his father, but he has taken to reading his Bible since he came to war.

Cpl. Meena wants me to come past Cleveland after the war and have a good old Syrian meal at his house. He said I wouldn't have to remember his name—just remember that his father was the only Syrian preacher in Cleveland, and find him that way.

One day I was walking through another olive orchard which held the Division Headquarters, and I noticed a soldier under a tree cleaning a sewing machine.

The soldier was Pfc. Leonard Vitale of Council Bluffs, Iowa. He's an old-timer in the Division. As I looked around, I saw a couple of other sewing machines sitting on boxes. "Good Lord, what are you doing?" I asked, "starting a sewing machine factory?"

Vitale said no, he was just getting set to do altering and mending for Division Headquarters. The first two sewing machines he had bought from Italians, and an AMGOT officer had given him the newest machine. It was a Singer and was set in an elaborate mahogany cabinet like a Victrola.

Vitale said he wasn't any expert tailor but did pick up some of the rudiments during the three and a half years he spent in the CCC, and thought he would do all right and make a little money on the side. As I walked away he called out: "I'll have this war sewed up in a couple of months."

★ ★ ★

Another story was floating around and wound up in *Stars and Stripes Weekly*:

A WAC convoy of three trucks made a rest stop

near a clump of trees. The WAC sergeant did not notice a nearby engineer work detail of about thirty GIs until the trucks were unloaded of WACs. Something had to be done. After an exchange of signals between the sergeants, the Engineer Sergeant, being a gentleman, gave the following commands—*FALL IN, AT-TENTION, ABOUT FACE*; then after the trucks had been reloaded, DISMISSED.

Once when Fred was invited to the Funnaris while they ate supper—they ate about nine in the evening and then went to bed—one thing he learned was that formerly a Fascist order forbade shaking hands, replacing that greeting with the typical Fascist hand salute. That explained the reason why, every time Fred came in or left, he had to go through the ceremony of shaking hands with every member of the family. Also, whenever any of them went into his room, from Mina up, they would always shake hands. Apparently, they did not like the old order.

While on a trip to several AA sites, the Captain stopped at a field shower unit for a hot shower. Enlisted men not only had a shower but also got a complete change of clothing—head to foot. Towels were also furnished. The shower unit could handle about 1,200 men per day. It was quite a setup, all in tents and trailers. Clothes were sterilized, washed and then issued out again.

The ranking medical officer of the Wing told the Captain that when the 64th first came into the Naples area the venereal disease problem was of such magnitude that he felt something drastic had to be done. He proceeded to rent a small hotel in Frattamagoire, planning to engage a group of prostitutes to be kept there in the building. He intended to give them a regular medical inspection and keep them clean. The plan probably would have worked and would have been quite successful. However, higher authority put a stop to it. What fun the press would have had back in the States if they were to learn of a setup like that. It probably would not have been so much fun either and would have really raised a stink.

★ ★ ★

The Army had quite a network of telephone lines, with each organization having its own switchboard or exchange. Some exchanges were quite large and, of course, there were many small ones. It would be most confusing if every unit's exchange would be called by its number, and also there would be the danger that anyone could keep track of the various unit locations. So each exchange had a name. Sometime the names and combinations of names were quite amusing. One exchange was Gorgeous and another was Underwear. Can you imagine asking for Gorgeous Underwear to locate a particular person? Another exchange that was quite large had a Forward and a Rear exchange. Both were run by WACs. It was a laugh to call a Forward exchange, ask for her Rear, and then have her tell you that it was busy.

★ ★ ★

One night in March, bridge was being played in Fred's room with Captain Butler, Signor Funnari, and the British officer Captain Hackforth-Jones who had the room next to Fred's. The British did not like the idea of just being one of the Jones boys, so they added on a name to distinguish themselves. Another British officer had the last name of Duncan-Smith.

★ ★ ★

Remember the interpreter? He finally got himself in trouble. He had been going around the community, more or less blackmailing the civilians. He would go to them and claim that he had quite a bit of authority with the U.S. Army and tell them that he could keep the Army from taking over their homes or buildings for official purposes. To get him to use his so-called influence, the people would give him various valuables or money. In some cases, officers were renting rooms and paying for them personally. He would come around and demand a part of the money back.

Charges were preferred against him when evidence had been obtained, and he was tried before an AMG (Allied Military Government) court. He did not get what he deserved, but he did lose his job as interpreter and was fined $30.00 plus a suspended six-month sentence.

* * *

The Early Warning section was beginning to get compliments on their work. Things seemed to be in good shape. Officers of the Fighter Wing Headquarters were beginning to hand out compliments to the Brigade Headquarters. Every little bit helped.

Convery had been working with the controllers and keeping them informed about the locations of various AA units. The controller would occasionally have a plane that was making an unidentified track. He would ask the AA officer on duty to try to find out whether any of the gun locations could give any information about that particular plane. Every once in awhile a gun unit would see the plane and be able to pass back the information regarding the markings, etc. through the lines. This really would help the controller because many times there would be unidentified tracks and the controller would be on pins and needles until the plane could be identified.

* * *

The Funnaris treated Fred to another nice dinner of spaghetti, meat, cauliflower with cheese, wine, and fruit (oranges and apples) for dessert. In Italy they ate their oranges and apples with a knife and fork, never touched by their fingers. The apples were cut in quarters first and then into small pieces like meat. To peel and eat an orange, the fork was stuck into the top or stem end of the orange, and then a ring was cut around the bottom by holding the orange upright on the fork. After that, the orange was cut into slices.

Apparently, it was not considered polite to touch your food. The maid even picked up the uneaten slices of bread with a fork.

Strangely, they ate their bread with their fingers and also wiped up their plate with the bread.

Newspaper clipping from *Stars & Stripes Weekly*, "The Roving Reporter" by Ernie Pyle, March 9, 1944:

IN ITALY—In my usual role of running other people's business, I've been threshing around with an idea. Honest. It's to give the combat soldier some little form of recognition more than he is getting now.

Everybody who serves overseas, no matter where or what he's doing, gets extra pay. Enlisted men get 20 percent additional, and officers 10 percent.

Airmen get an additional 50 percent above this for flight pay. As a result, officer-fliers get 60 percent above their normal base pay, and enlisted fliers, such as gunners and radio operators, get 70 percent.

All that is fine, and as it should be. But the idea I was toying with is why not give your genuine combat ground soldier something corresponding to flight pay. Maybe a good word for it would be "fight pay."

★ ★ ★

NO DISTINCTION

The idea being this—of any million men overseas, probably no more than 100,000 are in actual combat with the enemy. As it is now, there is no official distinction between the dogface lying for days and nights under constant mortar fire on an Italian hill and the Headquarters clerk living safely and comfortably in a hotel in Rio de Janeiro.

Their two worlds are so far apart the human mind can barely grasp the magnitude of the difference. One lives like a beast and dies in great numbers. The other is merely working away from home. Both are necessary and both are doing their jobs, but it seems to me the actual warrior deserves something to set him apart.

And medals are not enough.

★ ★ ★

PROUD CATEGORY

When I was at the front the last time, several infantry officers brought up this very same suggestion. They say combat pay would mean a lot to the fighting man. It would put him into a proud category and make him feel that somebody appreciates what he endures.

Obviously, no soldier would ever go into combat just to get extra "fight pay." That isn't the point. There is simply not enough money in the world to pay any single individual his due for battle suffering.

But it would put upon him a mark of distinction, a recognition that his miserable job was a royal one, and that the rest of us were aware of it. Or maybe I'm nuts, who knows?

Let's change the subject. One of the meanest stunts I've heard of is a Christmas envelope full of clippings a practical joker back home sent a soldier over here.

The clippings consisted of colored ads cut out of magazines—and they showed every luscious American thing from huge platters of ham-and-eggs on up to sport vacationers lolling in their bright bathing robes on the sand, surrounded by beautiful babes. Yep, there oughta be a law . . .

On second thought, I know even a meaner trick than that one. In fact, this one would take first prize in an ornery contest at any season, Christmas or otherwise. The worst is that it happened to a very front-line infantryman.

Some of his friends back home sent him three bottles of whiskey for Christmas. They came separately, were wonderfully packed, and the bottles came through without a break.

The first bottle tasted fine to the cold kids at the front. But when the second and third ones came, the boys found they had been opened and drained along the way, and then carefully resealed and continued on their journey.

Of course, mailing them in the first place was illegal, but that's beside the point. The point is that somewhere in the world there is a louse of a man with two quarts of whiskey inside him, who should have his worthless neck wrung off . . .

At one of our airdromes recently, a German plane sneaked over and dropped five-pronged steel spikes over the field. Our fliers called it a "jacks raid," since they resembled the "jacks" kids used to play with in school, only much bigger. These vicious spikes could puncture the tires when our planes taxied out.

So, the field engineers dug up a huge magnet, attached it to the front of a truck and swept the entire field free of the spikes. Then, they were immediately loaded onto our planes, and we flew over and dropped them back on the German airfields. There haven't been any "jack raids" since then . . .

There seemed to be an Italian trait which was seen in the adults as well as in the youngsters. So many times it was noticed that when one gave a youngster a piece of candy, he did not express gratitude and happiness for the gift but more of a glee for having been able to obtain it. He would immediately start asking for more. Adults were the same. The feeling was given that in the future the situation would be the same between nations, with the U.S. doing the giving and others doing the receiving, asking for more without regard for that which had already been received.

★ ★ ★

At a meal at the Funnaris, Mr. Funnari explained that it was an old custom for the head of the family to cut the bread at the head of the table. The bread was put on the table in the loaf. No plates were used. The loaves were round and quite large. The head of the family would hold the loaf under his left arm with a firm grip in his left hand and slice off the pieces.

The first time Fred started to leave the table, he folded his napkin. The napkins were about the size of tea towels. The girls stopped him and said that for a guest to fold his napkin meant that he never intended to come back.

Some people were thinking that the war would be over in just a month or two. But the Captain did not think there would be any chance of Germany collapsing. The war had a long way to go. It was anything but easy. He knew of companies of 250 men that only had about 25 men left of the original roster. The other 225 men were all replacements. The Captain had been under shell fire several times, and unless he had to, he had no desire to live under it 24 hours a day.

Once the Captain had to go to Brigade Headquarters. He met his long-time friend, Lt. Col. Neal McKay, who had some very interesting things to tell. The 439th had to make another move and, just as they were ready, Colonel Bowers got sick with pneumonia and had to go to the hospital. Colonel McKay took the outfit over on orders because Major Jones was not believed capable. When Fred visited with Neal McKay several weeks before, he told him of the Jones affair, and McKay was thankful because he had the whole picture. Neal was to go back to his own outfit because there was a higher Headquarters nearby that could keep an eye on the outfit while Bowers was in the hospital. When Convery first went into the National Guard in 1921 at Olympia, Washington, Neal McKay was a young 2nd lieutenant.

It had been almost a year since the landing at Oran, Algeria. One of the procedures was the compiling of lists of people who were recommended for rotation back to the States. Many of the officers who were on the lists deserved to go back. However, it seemed that, in a lot of cases, those recommended were officers who had dissatisfied their commanders. That really created a lot of dissension. That was the procedure used to send Jones back to the States.

About the middle of March, Convery heard about a massive plan to bomb Monte Casino. At Monte Casino was a monastery up on a mesa of solid rock. It was at the head of a valley and was a very strong strategic point for the Germans. The monastery had many cellars in the huge rock, along with passageways, etc. The Germans had taken over the mountain and fortified it with many guns. The mount gave them the advantage of height for observation and firing purposes and it was a real obstacle. The Army had avoided any damage to the monastery for political reasons, even though there was considerable fighting all around the area. The mount with its monastery just could not be taken or passed because of the heavy artillery installed on it.

Plans were made to hit Monte Casino with as many air strikes as possible. The 64th Fighter Wing was to furnish fighter cover and also fighter bombers. Heavy bombers were to come from a number of bases in Europe, England, and Africa. It seemed like enough to destroy the entire mountain. One of Convery's trips took him to an AA Battalion Headquarters in the Casino valley located in an olive grove up on a knoll. From there he could see Monte Casino.

His route (planned from a map) took him up the center of the valley to a crossroad and then due east to the AA Headquarters. The people at the Headquarters asked him how he got there. He told them, and they said that they never used that road in the daytime because trucks or traffic of any kind drew artillery fire. Apparently, one jeep was not worth firing upon.

When he got back, he contacted the Brigade Headquarters and got word to Brigade Commander General Paul B. Kelly to go to the AA Battalion Headquarters he had visited during the day. He recommended to the General that he go that night in order to be there the next morning at daylight. He could not pass any other information over the phone but the General knew what was being said to him because two days before Convery had told him that there was going to be a raid and gave him some indication about the size of the attack. General Kelly went up to the Battalion Headquarters that night, and the next morning he saw one of the biggest and largest bombings of the war from a grandstand seat. However, Jerry was not knocked out. They just went down into the tunnels and waited out the bombings. The Monte Casino was never taken. It had to be bypassed.

Convery had a long day the day before, had been up all night, and just couldn't make the trip again. He was always sorry he didn't make the extra effort to go see the show.

★ ★ ★

Convery made a trip to Brigade Headquarters and then to 5th Army Headquarters. Brigade did not have the command of all the AA in Italy anymore. He was okay and the personnel at 5th Army Headquarters seemed to be well satisfied and did not want to see any changes made in the Early Warning procedures. He asked for another officer so that he would not have to take a shift in the Control Room. He really had been doing two different jobs. He had been using what time he could to make trips around to AA units, which was all on his own time while still doing duty at the Control Room. He felt pretty good about it all. With the new arrangements, all the main AA units of the 5th Army were tied together, both with wire and radio telephone. The AA units were receiving and giving information to the Wing, and the Wing officers appreciated the connections with the AA for their assistance. He was also told that he could have transportation any time he needed it.

The Early Warning from the Wing was beginning to show real results and ranking officers were talking about it. When Convery went to the Wing Headquarters, the section did not amount to anything. The section became a smooth working team of four officers and four enlisted men. The Colonel of an AA group gave credit to the Early Warning setup for furnishing information that made it possible to knock down a number of Jerry planes. Convery felt good about that and that he had earned his salary for the year.

★ ★ ★

Fred bought Esta a pair of Wedgewood cups and saucers. They were not particularly beautiful, but they were very old. They were the old-style blue, distinctly Italian in style, as though the Wedgewood people had made them for the Italian trade. As an indication of their age, the saucers were turned up nearly straight on the sides, like the saucer of a flower pot. At one time, saucers were used to drink out of, for cooler coffee.

★ ★ ★

While on duty in the Ops, or Operations Room, it was very interesting to listen to the radio conversations just before and during a dog fight. It was strange, but most of the time the pilots were very calm and talked in the most matter-of-fact way. One was heard to say, "There they are (Jerry planes) down there. Let's go down." Then there were times they reported that they had been hit and that they were bailing out. After that you didn't hear any more.

★ ★ ★

Newspaper clipping from *Stars & Stripes Weekly*, March 28, 1944:

"FRONT-LINE FLASHES"

Fighting men who consistently have been fed hash, meat and stew can't be blamed for not seeing eye-to-eye with the glib advertisements of these products. So it wasn't surprising to see the enthusiasm which greeted the arrival of a quarter cow "accidentally" killed during German shelling. With the problem of butchering confronting the hungry dogfaces, Pvt. Gordon N. Fair of Kittanning, Pennsylvania; Pvt. William E. Cramer of East McKeesport, Pennsylvania; Pvt. Raymond Dugan of Campbellsburg, Kentucky; and Sgt. Richard C. Woolsen of Glenside, Pennsylvania, immediately began work. Their tools, which replaced the standard butcher's equipment, included a hunting knife, a jack-knife and a bayonet. With homemade meat grinders produced by Cpl. Walter Anglade of New York City, the boys turned out hamburgers, not like their mothers' but mighty good anyway.

★ ★ ★

On March 30, 1944, Captain Convery was no longer an orphan without a home. He was assigned to the 5th Army AA Command (Army Headquarters). He was happy because, before, he was in a rather unstable position in a replacement pool, and by some odd quirk, he might have had any sort of an assignment.

General Rutledge of the AA Brigade went to the 64th Fighter Wing Headquarters and asked General Hawkins of the Fighter Wing to have Convery attached as the AA officer on the Wing staff. But the staff was filled, and it couldn't be done. The Table of Organization called for only a certain number of officers. Anyway, it was nice to know what General Rutledge wanted to do, because on the Wing Table of Organization it called for a lieutenant colonel as the AA officer.

★ ★ ★

Newspaper clipping from *Stars & Stripes Weekly*, London, March 29, 1944:

"WACS SMOKING IN PUBLIC OK'D"

Although smoking on streets and other public places is outlawed for British girls in the Auxiliary Territorial Service, ETOUSA officials today announced they planned no similar rule against smoking by WACs.

Under a new order, ATS girls, counterpart of American WACs, are not allowed to smoke in many public places. Male members of the British Army may light up when they please.

ETOUSA officials said they expected the WACs to observe the tenets of good judgment but as "members of the U.S. Army we desire to treat them as we treat men. As our soldiers are permitted to smoke in streets, WACs are naturally given the same privileges."

★ ★ ★

Newspaper clipping from *Stars & Stripes Weekly*, March 30, 1944:

"LOST NURSES RETURN SAFE"

Advanced Allied Headquarters, March 29—Three American nurses, who have wandered about German-held Albania for months since the plane they were in was forced down there last November, have been rescued and are safe and unharmed in Allied territory, it was disclosed here today.

The repatriated nurses are 2nd Lts. Helen Porter, Hanksville, Utah; Ava Ann Maness, Paris, Texas; and Wilma Dale, Butler, Kentucky. All other occupants of the plane escaped from Albania in January.

The nurses' story began when a plane full of medical personnel used on air evacuation mission planes took off from Sicily and headed for Italy. The weather was bad, and when the plane broke through the clouds, the pilot didn't know where he was. He spotted an airfield and started to land. But when he found he was being fired upon, he pulled away. Two Messerschmitts chased him and he shook them by diving into some clouds. Later he made a forced landing on an ordinary field.

The nurses were never in German hands. They were befriended by Albanian patriots who hid them from the Nazis and passed them through the underground.

★ ★ ★

Newspaper clipping from *Stars & Stripes Weekly*, "The Roving Reporter" by Ernie Pyle, March 30, 1944:

WITH THE 5TH ARMY BEACHHEAD FORCES

You've read about the little Cub planes that fly slowly around over the front lines doing artillery spotting for us. They're a wonderful little branch of the service, and the risks they take are tremendous.

The Germans try to shoot them down with ack-ack, and occasionally a German fighter will sneak in and take a pass at them. But the Cub is so slow that the fighters usually overshoot, and the Cub can drop down and land immediately.

The saddest story I've ever heard about a Cub happened on the Fifth Army Beachhead. One Long Tom—or 155-rifle—was the unwitting villain in this case.

This certain gun fired only one shell that entire day—but that one shell, with all the big sky to travel in, made a direct hit on one of our Cubs in the air, and blew it all to smithereens. It was just one of those incredible one-in-ten-billion possibilities, but it happened.

Ernie Pyle continues:

In the column the other day about our horrible experience when the war correspondents' villa was bombed, I said that after it was over I didn't feel shaky nor nervous.

Since then little memories of the bombing have gradually come back into my consciousness. I recall now that I went to take my pocket comb out of my shirt pocket to comb my hair, but instead actually took my handkerchief out of my hip pocket and started combing my hair with the handkerchief.

And, at noon, I realized I had smoked a whole pack of cigarettes since 7:30 a.m.

Me nervous? Why I should say not.

The day before the bombing I got a little package of chewing gum and life-savers and what not. I tore the return address off the package and put it on my table in order to write a note of thanks to the sender.

The package and address were both lost in the bombing. All I remember is that it was from Spencer, Iowa. So will whoever sent it, please accept my thanks?

I've spoken of soldiers' wartime pets so many times you're probably bored with the subject. But here's one more, regardless.

The Headquarters of a certain tank regiment where I have many friends had a beautiful police dog named Sergeant. He belonged to everybody, was a lovable dog, liked to go through a whole repertoire of tricks, and was almost human in his sensitiveness.

He had even become plane-raid conscious, and when he heard planes in the sky would run and get in his own private foxhole—or any foxhole, if he were away from home.

"Sergeant" was dutifully in his foxhole yesterday when he died. Shrapnel from an air burst got him. He wasn't killed instantly, and they had to destroy him.

The outfit lost two officers, four men and a dog in that raid. It is not belittling the men who died to say Sergeant's death shared a high place in the grief of those who are left.

★ ★ ★

On most of Fred's trips to the AA units he would be gone all day. He would leave about eight in the morning and not get back until around eight in the evening. He would be riding in a jeep all day. The nickname for a jeep, Fannybuster, was no exaggeration. One day he went by Brigade Headquarters, and while there inquired for mail. He got a couple of newspapers and a package from Esta, number 25, with caramels, Vienna sausages, clams and Lorna Doone cookies. The mail clerk saw the numbers on the packages Esta sent and he said, "Captain, here is the 25th."

Lt. Russell was with Fred in the mountains most of the afternoon, and toward evening they began to get hungry. Russell said, "Convery, why don't you break open that package and see what OUR wife sent?"

He had a room at the same place as Fred and got a big kick out of the packages that Esta sent. His wife seldom sent him anything. When Esta asked for suggestions for things to send, he said, "For God's sake, what are you waiting for?" He was from Tennessee and loved to eat. He told everyone that Fred had a small PX.

To get back to the story, they were hungry, so while traveling Fred opened the packages. In the mountains they had Lorna Doone cookies, Vienna sausages and caramels. The packages were shared with the driver. They stopped in a village and bought some almonds to finish off with.

The almonds were 60 lira a kila. A kila is about two pounds. The almonds there were tougher and harder than almonds in the States. The only possible way to crack them was to put them on the floor of the jeep and hit them with the butt end of their 45s.

★ ★ ★

In April, Fred's turn came up for a trip to a rest camp. Rest cure, it was called. He left one morning with a Major Henry for Naples to leave by boat for the camp on the Isle of Capri. They were driven to Naples in Henry's civilian car. The car was one that had been confiscated by the French and left behind when the French unit went to the front, leaving the car in a civilian garage. When it was found with OD paint, GI tires, and apparently no owner, the Wing picked it up. About the time they returned from the rest camp, the French had returned from the front and started looking for their car. Major Henry had to turn it over to them because they had it first. He was certainly mad because his boys had just finished doing a lot of work on it to get it in good running shape. To take one of those civilian cars and get it in good running shape required not only an expert mechanic but a magician as well.

★ ★ ★

They arrived at Rest Camp Headquarters in Naples about 10:30 a.m., and by the time the arrangements were settled, it was about 11:00. They had nothing to do but wander around and look in the shop windows. Most of the stores were closed because it was Sunday. Before they left by boat, they wandered around for an hour. On the way they saw that up the street there was quite a bit of activity at a bombed out building. It was one of several buildings that had been bombed a few nights before. The workers were still searching for bodies.

The buildings were not built like the ones at home. Everything was constructed without the benefit of bricks or concrete and with the minimum of girders. The walls were of soft stone with dirt filled in between, making the wall about two feet thick. Dirt was mixed with lime and cement to make a binder instead of with sand to hold the stone. Consequently, when a building was hit by a bomb, it collapsed into one big pile of dirt and individual stones. The walls did not hold together as they would if they were brick and concrete. Fred had noticed those piles of dirt at every bombed building and at first wondered where it all came from, but when he saw some construction going on, he understood.

That particular building was an apartment building that seemed to have been sheared off so that you could look into the rooms of each floor, like looking into a child's doll house except that it was an apartment house. This has been mentioned before.

The rooms were identical on each floor. It made a person feel that he was looking into the privacy of several families by being able to look right into what had been their bathrooms and bedrooms with everything, strange as it may seem, as it was when the bomb fell, even the pictures on the wall.

A group of men were working in the rubble. Major Henry and Fred elbowed their way through the crowd and saw that the workmen were just removing a woman who had been in the building. The body seemed to have been caught in such a way that they were having difficulty. As they shoveled away the dirt, an Army cot and overcoat made their appearance. The men did not have time to wait around to see what else was going to show up, but you can draw your own conclusions.

★ ★ ★

They arrived at the Isle of Capri late in the afternoon and had to ride up on a *funicular* to the shopping and hotel area. Major Henry and Convery were settled in their rooms. Before going to supper, they went to the bar for awhile and absorbed some liquid punishment. The bar was a very popular place. Most of the officers accumulated there for a time before going to the dining room. No money was allowed at the bar. Payment was made by a coupon system. A book of coupons with varying values could be purchased at the desk for $5.00.

After a couple of drinks, he and Major Henry went in to eat. Although the meals were not planned with the idea of gorging anyone, there was plenty. The supplies from which the meals were prepared were strictly GI, and the chefs at the hotel certainly had the knack of making food taste far better than at the officers' mess. Soup was served every evening and it was usually delicious. Powdered eggs were turned into a remarkably fine custard for dessert.

The tables were all set for varying numbers—some for two, others three, four, and up to eight. As the men went into the dining room, they were met by a headwaiter in tails which gave the impression that they were of utmost importance. Fred had seen a number of headwaiters, but never before had seen one who was quite as stiff as this one. The only time any part of him moved in a separate motion from the rest of his body (outside of his legs when he walked) were his hands and arms when he bowed and beckoned you to a certain table. Fred was actually fascinated, watching to see whether he ever turned his head without turning his body. He was never able to catch him. He reminded one of a clothespin, dressed up like a doll.

During every meal, except breakfast, music was provided by a three-piece orchestra— violin, accordion, and guitar. Sometimes a singer would join them. Though the spring flowers were not out yet, sprigs of blossoms of some kind were always on the tables. After dinner, Major Henry and Fred walked down to another hotel where a movie was being shown. They sat through it for two hours and then returned to their hotel. Sat through it is correct because it was cold. There was no heat whatsoever. By the time the show was over, it was time to go to bed.

Fred slept until after 8:00 the next morning and then went down to breakfast. He did not shave because there was no hot water. For breakfast he had something that was in the nature of a hot cake but much thinner and rubbery. He told the waiter that he did not care much for it, and the waiter shrugged his shoulders and said, "Just crepes." Fred thought that crepes must be rather plebeian to Europeans. The famous Crepes Suzette that he had paid up to $1.75 for in the so-called French restaurant (Arnold's) were nothing more or less than a poor hot cake used as a wick to burn up some good brandy.

Because he had not shaved, he felt rather unkempt and headed for the barber shop immediately after breakfast. He had a shave, haircut, and a manicure, the first he had since he arrived overseas. Major Henry and a friend of his, a Captain Thompson, were waiting for Fred to get shorn. As soon as he was out of the chair, they headed down toward the center of activity to see the sights.

★ ★ ★

Major Henry, Captain Thompson, and Fred started out to see a very famous place called the Blue Grotto. They were very fortunate as far as weather was concerned because, at that time of the year, the weather was undependable and bad weather was not a good time to see the Blue Grotto.

To go to the Blue Grotto, they first had to go down the hill to water level to hire a boat. Going down the hill was quite an event in itself if one uses what is called the *funicular*— a cable railway whose starting point was the square on top and the other terminal was at the street along the waterfront. There were two cars, and while one went up, the other went down, counterbalancing each other with a switching arrangement midway between for the two cars to pass. Because the hill was very steep, the cars reminded them of a section of steps on wheels, with each step arranged with a bench on each side for the passengers on one side to face the passengers on the other side of the step. Each car had about six such steps. They were sitting opposite an elderly Italian whose English was as limited as their Italian. However, he was able to let them know that this very famous Short Line railroad was the subject of a very popular Italian song. Because they didn't ask for services rendered, they saw no reason for handing out well-earned money for a tip. The tune went like this, "Da da, da da, da de da de da, Funiculee, Funiculaa, Funiculee, Funiculaa," etc. Fred learned afterward from the Funnaris that *funicula* and *funiculi* did not mean anything, but the Italian explained by his motions that one meant *up* and the other meant *down*. In any event, it was fun because he explained it all and sang the song all the way down. At the time, they did not know that he was building them up for a tip, but they found out as soon as they got off at the bottom, because he followed them along for about a block, trying to talk the American millionaire suckers into giving him a tip.

Along the beach, a boatman was located who had a power

launch that would take them to the Blue Grotto for a fee of $5.00, or a dollar apiece if there were more than five persons. They could not see paying out the five bucks for just the three, so they waited a few minutes. Along came an infantry officer with two British nurses in tow, who were just there for the day and wanted to see as much as they could in a short while. When "in tow" is used it means exactly that, because both of them were quite large and one of them reminded one of Kate Smith.

They started out along the coastline and enjoyed the ride because the cliffs and rocks were really beautiful. The water was a wonderful blue and there was a slight swell. On the way back, Major Henry, whose home state was Oklahoma, demonstrated that he had been brought up riding horses and not in small boats.

No one had the slightest idea what the Blue Grotto was except that it was some sort of a cave that one entered while remaining in the boat and that it was reputed to be very beautiful. Actually, it turned out to be exactly that but far different from what was imagined. When they arrived at the entrance, all that could be seen was a dark hole in the side of a steep cliff. Bobbing all around in front were a number of rowboats, manned by Italians, who were standing up to do their rowing and who were keeping their boats nosed into the swell. In that part of the world, there was very little rise and fall to the tide. Consequently, the opening into the Blue Grotto was never much larger or smaller at any time, with the exception that, if there was any swell at all, the entrance became covered over, making it impossible to enter. They transferred to the small boats—Major Henry and Captain Thompson into one, the infantry officer and one British nurse into another, and that left Fred with Kate Smith.

For the rowboat to get into the grotto, it was necessary to wait around outside until the swell was just right and then start in when the water was lower and provided a large opening. The opening was not wide enough to permit the use of oars. A chain had been fastened along the side of the opening for the boatman to pull the boat inside. While they were being pulled in, the swell came up behind. After perfect timing by the boatman, the boat almost shot in, in much the same manner as though it were a surfboard.

Before they started in, the boatman made Kate Smith and Fred lie down on the bottom of the boat, below the level of the sides of the rowboat. He did likewise but at the same time pulled the boat in by pulling on the chain. Major Henry said that his boatman did not time it quite right and almost got squeezed between the edge of the boat and the roof of the entrance. Squeezing apparently was a part of entering the grotto, because Kate Smith and Fred were squeezed tight in the bow. Inside, the water was perfectly still and the color of blue rinse water when washing clothes, except that it was full of light. The boatman would pull his oar through the water, and the combination of the light blue water and air bubbles was beautiful. Along the sides and in the shadows, phosphorus could be seen. He rowed around the grotto once, and then he waited a few moments for the right time to get out. While waiting, the surf could be heard outside. One could not help but wonder what would happen if a strong wind should suddenly come up, preventing the boats from getting out.

The grotto was a large cave that had been washed out by the action of the water. One might imagine that it would have been perfectly dark inside, but it was not. The cliff had been washed away below the water level on the seaward side, and the sunlight came up through the water casting a blue light all over the inside.

★ ★ ★

The next morning they made a trip by automobile to another part of the island and saw what at one time had been the home and villa of Caesar Augustus Tiberias. It was really very interesting. The ruins were much the same as the ruins of Pompeii although not so extensive. There was one place nearby where the cliff dropped off straight down to the sea with rocks along the shoreline. At this point, the emperor used to throw prisoners and

Christians over, reportedly, just to hear them scream on the way down to the rocks.

To get up to the place required either a hike or a ride on a jackass. They decided to ride the jackasses. Going up was not too bad. An Italian was sent along to keep the jackasses moving. When he would hit them over the rump with a stick, they put on additional speed, which did not bother a bit. But, coming down, it started to rain, and the stone steps, already worn quite smooth, became a little slippery. Frankly, it was not too enjoyable to be riding an animal going down slippery steps with an Italian behind berating it with a stick. The Italian kept beating the jackass with his stick to make it go faster. It would get ahead of him and then slow up. As soon as he caught up with it and hit it again, it would speed up. Both the jackasses and the Italian must have known what they were doing because all three got back all right without any accident.

The rain continued the rest of that day and the next. Outside of doing some shopping, and looking around in the shops, not much was done. The streets were really no wider than an average sidewalk and, of course, had no motorized traffic. This was when Fred bought most of the things he sent home.

* * *

When the Rest Camp at Naples was first used, it was thought that there was enough water to last throughout the whole season. There were no wells or springs on the island. The only supply of water was from rain water and water that was shipped over by boat. They had not planned for the extravagant use by the Americans. Consequently, the place had to be closed for several months until the supply could be replenished, and then drastic rationing was established. There was no hot water in the hotels except on Wednesdays and Saturdays. There were signs all over the hotel asking that water not be used excessively and that the guests refrain from flushing toilets more than necessary.

The night before Fred was to leave, he found a note in his room informing him that his stay was up and that he would be called at 7:00 in the morning in order to have breakfast before departure time. The boat would leave the dock at 8:30. The departure was handled in much the same manner as arrival except that it was early in the morning for that place, and very few people were up and around. The ride back was on a smaller boat and quite crowded.

He was glad he went when he did, because it was most miserable during the next week or so. Vesuvius had started to erupt, and because the ash was carried for hundreds of miles, the place became covered with about an inch or two of ash..

In the first part of April everyone was hoping that they would be moving forward, because when the warm weather started, they were sure the flies were going to be terrible. While talking to the squadron surgeon about it, he agreed. He said that the sewers around there were run into open ditches and then out into the fields and vineyards.

When he was on the way back from Brigade, Fred stopped to take a look at an Italian sawmill. The logs were being sawed by hand. Two men had an 18-inch log up on a platform and were pulling a saw back and forth, sawing the log into planks. One was above and the other was under, using a saw about six feet long.

Fred had been doing a lot of riding in a jeep. He kept a journal and was averaging about 2,500 miles a month in jeep travel over the rough Italian roads. When riding in a jeep, his right foot would rest on the cutout part of the body. Along the side of the jeep was a safety belt across the opening to keep the passenger from being thrown out in case there was a bad bump. He rode all day with his foot in the cutout part, his leg and knee braced against the strap, thus developing a corn on the side of his foot.

★ ★ ★

It seems there was a convoy that had been spotted by a Jerry plane. In order to keep track of the convoy, the plane started circling, just out of range of the guns. When the plane's gas started running low, another plane began the circling. Finally, when someone determined the Jerry's radio frequency, they called him and told him to go in the other direction because "he was driving them crazy." The pilot of the Jerry plane replied OK and swung right around and circled in the other direction.

★ ★ ★

Languages were quite a problem, just the same as in Africa. But no one ever dreamed that there would be trouble with the English. The British terms were so different that it was almost like learning another language. For example, a truck was a *lorry*; gasoline was *petrol*; kerosene was *paraffin*. The French called gasoline *essence*, and the Italians called gasoline *benzene*. The British and the Americans, through their two Headquarters, made an agreement: If the Americans would call gasoline *petrol*, the British would call their lorries *trucks*.

★ ★ ★

Convery previously mentioned that General Rutledge asked General Hawkins to have him transferred to the Wing and that it could not be done because the Table of Organization did not provide for another officer. Then he was transferred to the AA section of the 5th Army Headquarters. In the meantime, the recommendation for promotion of Major Selby to lieutenant colonel to fill the vacancy of AA officer at the Wing had been submitted. He heard the recommendation had bounced back and had bounced hard, because promotions in one branch could not be given to officers of another. So, the opening was still there for an officer with a grade of lieutenant colonel.

★ ★ ★

A group of officers from the Wing had occasion to fly to Cairo. They saw the pyramids and even had a chance to fly on to the Holy Land and saw many of the sights there. One of the nice things was that they were able to bring back 180 dozen eggs, at 30 cents a dozen. The going price for eggs around Naples was 12 to 15 cents each, and eggs were not supposed to be bought. On the streets they were offered at 25 cents each.

★ ★ ★

While on his way once to the Operations Room, Fred passed an interesting situation. Several little girls were skipping rope in the street—using a long rope with two of them swinging it. The girls must have been between six and ten years old. Right in the middle of the group was a lanky, six-foot soldier. A good bet would be that he had at least two little sisters at home. The girls were swinging the rope, and he was doing the jumping. You might think he would have been embarrassed, but he wasn't one bit. Not only was he not embarrassed, but the other soldiers watching had amused looks on their faces and at the same time looked a bit envious.

★ ★ ★

Jerry paid us a visit, and it wasn't with peanuts.

★ ★ ★

The Captain's responsibilities grew in tremendous proportions, and at times he got rather weary. A Brigadier General and a Major, both of them British, visited him. There were British units under the 64th Fighter Wing as well as American, and they wanted to know about the Early Warning information coming from the Wing operation.

A meeting was called of all of the S-2s (Intelligence Officers) of several AA Brigades and groups. It all concerned the Early Warning end of the AA activity. Captain Convery was going to be on the spot, not from anything gone wrong but because they were vitally interested. Because the Early Warning procedure was going so well, everyone was sticking his fingers into the setup as results were beginning to show. The procedures that had been set up for the Early Warning to the Anti-Aircraft guns were really working and seemed to be the answer for a service that was badly needed. At the meeting many questions were asked. Everyone appeared to be satisfied.

★ ★ ★

Italian moonlit nights were beautiful but nobody liked to see such bright moonlight. Those nights were good for air raids. The Wing Headquarters had been fortunate not to have very many. One raid, however, was quite disturbing. A show was being put on by Irving Berlin called *It's the Army*. It was really good and included a cast comprised of all GI soldiers. Just before the last act, an alert was sounded, lights were put out, and the whole theater was dark. Flashlights came on from all over, and the show was finished by the aid of the flashlights. Irving Berlin came on the stage and led community singing with the aid of the flashlights until the alert was over. Berlin must have been scared because, hardly knowing what to say, he said over and over again not to be worried and for everyone to stay in his seat. Fred admitted that the one thing he wanted to do was to get out of there. The GI audience sat there for over an hour while the cast gave an impromptu bit of entertainment.

During the air raid a bomb was dropped on a rope factory that had been taken over and was being used as a barracks for the enlisted men of Headquarters. The bomb, about four feet high and a foot in diameter, lodged itself in the building but did not explode. The factory was about two blocks from the theater. It sure would have been messy had it not been a dud.

★ ★ ★

Things were moving along toward the Captain's assignment with the Wing as AA Officer. He had his fingers crossed because there were so many places where things could go wrong. He was told at Brigade Headquarters that 5th Army Headquarters was very anxious to have him on the Wing staff. The Adjutant of the 64th told him that it was okay with General Barcus. However, General Barcus (who replaced General Hawkins) wanted to talk to General Bradshaw of the 5th Army AA command. He talked to Army Headquarters and was told that the Wing had already called the GI section to find out how to go about requesting the transfer.

Convery went up to Brigade, and one of the officers he knew told him that he had heard General Rutledge say that he had done work that no other AA officer had done and that they were lieutenant colonels in several cases.

When a mere Captain had two Generals thinking that he was good, it was really something to be proud of. Actually he didn't think he was as good as they did, but far be it from him to tell them anything different. It was just that he could see that certain things had to be done and did them without asking any questions. Fortunately, they turned out all right. He was in a position where there was a lot to be done and was given the go-ahead signal to do as he saw fit.

One time a humorous incident was heard over the RT (Radiotelephone). One fighter pilot was on the deck (flying low) and the rest of the flight was flying top cover (quite high). Two MEs (Jerry planes) got on his tail, and the low-lying pilot called for some help. The boys flying high did not want to come down and lose their altitude. One of them said over the RT, "Charlie is a fraidy cat—Charlie is a fraidy cat." Of course, the pilot on the deck pulled up and rejoined his flight because he knew the others wouldn't come down.

Wing Headquarters moved forward twice and everyone else was on the move. There was no end of grief to keep in contact with everyone and all units. Even so, contact was lost. Jerry was surely on the move. Headquarters was bivouacked in a former Jerry area. It was a nice area in trees and under cover. While they were quite far behind the front, they were a long way into former Jerry country.

★ ★ ★

Driving in new territory, Convery saw to it that his driver did not get off the roads. They never knew where the mines were going to be and with things moving as fast as they were, it was impossible to find them all. Two Signal Corps boys were blown off a cliff when one of them picked up something. No one knew what was picked up. It could have been a pencil or some other innocent looking booby trap. Jerry left all kinds of things behind that were booby-trapped—clothing or anything that could be rigged to explode when picked up. The two were way up in the hills. The roads and shoulders were continually swept for mines and were quite safe. For some protection Fred had sandbags on the floor and underneath the seat of his jeep.

★ ★ ★

Newspaper clipping from *Stars & Stripes Weekly*, May 13, 1944:

"FLASHES FROM THE ITALIAN FRONT LINES"

With just three bursts of three seconds each, 1st Lt. John J. Lenihan, Manchester, Connecticut, a P-47 pilot, bagged three Nazi planes in three minutes. And his three comrades got three more. The four Thunderbolts, on their way home from a strafing mission over Rome, ran into eleven German cargo planes and had a real field day.

For a time, an American lieutenant leading a recent combat patrol didn't know whether he was living in this world or the next. First, he was hit in the chest with a German grenade. He fell, severely wounded, and his tommy gun was knocked several yards away. As if that wasn't enough, he had to play dead when a German soldier crawled up to look at him. When the German left, the lieutenant began a two-mile crawling, stumbling trip back to an American aid station. On the way he hit a trip wire, setting off an entire string of German booby traps. He hit the dirt until the fireworks were over, and then he made it to safety.

Because the wounded German prisoner claimed he was in great pain and was unable to walk, the American litter squad was carrying him to the rear on a stretcher. "Then we ran into a heavy artillery barrage," relates Pvt. Marion Cox, litterman from Ft. Wayne, Indiana. "That damn Jerry was off the stretcher before we could set it down. When the barrage lifted, he climbed back on again. He didn't stay long though, brother."

Did you ever hear the story about the Jerry who wanted to surrender but had a hard time doing so because his pants kept falling down? It happened when Pvt. Ernest Ross, Old Orchard Beach, Maine, was bringing in a group of prisoners. Suddenly one of them dropped his hands and grabbed his pants. "Get them hands up," yelled Ross, waving his tommy gun. Jerry did that right quick, but down plopped his pants again. His belt was busted. So the German shuffled along, stopping periodically to reach for his pants while Ross periodically threatened him with his tommy gun.

For two nights, an American patrol had been searching the enemy lines for a troublesome machine gun nest. On the third night, Sgt. Albert J. Tetreaut, Meriden, Connecticut, the patrol leader, was about to give up the hunt when he received some unexpected help. "Is that you, Hans?" said a German voice nearby. The voice turned out to belong to the man with the machine gun. The situation, said Tetreaut, resulted favorably for the Allies.

★ ★ ★

At first the Early Warning section at Wing Headquarters was working with just the one Brigade of Anti-Aircraft Artillery. By

May they were also getting the information out to two British Brigades of Anti-Aircraft Artillery.

★ ★ ★

Attached, or rather with, the British troops, there was a unit of African Negroes who came from somewhere in the interior of Africa. They were tall fellows and did not use regular uniforms but had turbans and long robes. They were really fierce fighters with a reputation for never taking prisoners.

★ ★ ★

Fred was invited to a birthday party with the Funnaris. The party was a lot of fun. After the Funnaris had their dinner, they invited him in to share Papa's birthday cake. Their birthday cakes were not at all like ours but were like a pie. In fact, it could have been called a sort of cream pie with a crust made similar to the kind that is made with graham crackers. It was very good. He had wine which was served with every meal with the exception of breakfast. After they had the cake, Papa Funnari opened a bottle of champagne, served in silver champagne cups. Before Fred went in, he got Santino and the girls together and taught them *Happy Birthday to You*, and they sang to him while they had the champagne. Although the words were right, they were not very close to the tune, and they were not together. Even so, he liked it.

Captain Jones, the British officer who roomed next to Fred, came in afterward, and after talking awhile, they played a game similar to *Who Has the Thimble?*. However, in that game, a large string was tied in a loop and through a ring. Everyone sat in a close circle grasping the string loosely. The person who was *IT* turned his back and, upon returning, had to determine who had the ring. While doing that, everyone in the circle kept his hands moving back and forth and from side to side pretending to keep the person that was *IT* from seeing him. The ring was also passed along, and the person who was *IT* tried to name the person who had the ring. If he was successful, the person who had the ring became *IT*. After making a mistake and naming the wrong person, he had to give a forfeit. They covered the eyes of the person re-deeming the forfeit and asked him a question. Before the first question was asked, it was determined by motions what the act would be. For example, it could be a slap, caress, kiss, or tweak, which was just about the same as a pinch but with a twist. Each question was asked—by whom, how many, and where. There was much shouting and laughter, mostly in Italian, but they were learning to speak some English and all got along fine.

★ ★ ★

Every day or so some officer from one of the units that was re-ceiving information from us would come to see what we were doing so that he would understand better what was being received from us and be able to know what we wanted from his unit.

★ ★ ★

The mess at Headquarters was not what it could have been. The mess officer was a hard-working lieutenant but just did not know what to do to make the mess good or else he did not have the cooks. Convery didn't think it was the cooks, because if the mess officer knew his stuff, he could get the cooks to fix things the right way. They seemed to fix the foods the easiest way, which was to just heat them up as they came out of the can.

★ ★ ★

The mess officer told a story about trying to buy some local produce. He went into a yard and was met by the farmer. First the farmer shooed all of his daughters and his wife inside before he would talk to him and then told the mess officer he did not have a thing. There was produce around there, but the people were suspicious of us. They were afraid that it would be taken away from them without recompense.

★ ★ ★

Fred was certainly getting his laundry done nicely. It was done by the sister and mother of Caramella, the maid for the Funnaris. The sister who had four children did the washing, and the mother did the ironing. The sister had quite a hard time getting along because she lost her husband in the war up in Russia. Every once in awhile Fred gave some of his candy to Caramella to give to her sister's children. The mother was quite old, and the ironing was quite difficult. Caramella indicated that the ironing was very hard on Mama's wrists. All ironing was done with irons that were heated over charcoal fires. Some of the tailors' irons had a space between the bottom of the iron and the handle into which burning charcoal was put to keep the irons hot. Caramella's sister and mother did a beautiful job of ironing. The starch Esta sent helped a lot.

★ ★ ★

On May 29 the big push was on. The front was moving rapidly. Captain Convery had to keep in touch with the various AA units and went continuously from around 8:00 in the morning until after dinner time at night. He was putting in a lot of miles in a jeep.

★ ★ ★

Fred noticed something rather different in Italy. All of the babies seemed to be listless. Other places babies were always crying, or at least part of the time. It came to him that he never heard a baby crying. Lord knows there were enough of them. There were youngsters everywhere. Another thing was that they were never very active. Youngsters up to about three or four sat on their sister's or mother's laps without squirming a bit. He saw them sitting perfectly still for long periods while an older sister would be looking through their hair for lice. He seldom saw them playing, running or laughing. A command car or a jeep could be driven through the narrow streets fairly fast and never have to worry about a youngster running out in front of the vehicle. The streets could be filled with people, streets so narrow that individuals had to stand with their backs against a wall of a building to let one car through. No one seemed to have the energy to run in front of a car. The reason must have been that they ate practically nothing but vegetables and starches. It was a funny country. Ten thousand people took up about as much space as the business district of a small American community.

★ ★ ★

One evening in June, when Fred was walking down the main street of Frattamagoire, he observed that a great number of people were hanging beautiful bedspreads from their balconies. They were mostly of silk and in all colors. Some were of velvet, with rich designs and shades. Others were of lace, with bright silk underneath. Some were of silk and had painted pictures on them. He could not figure it out. When he returned to his room, he asked Maria, and she told him that it was a religious occasion in which the people hung out their bedspreads in respect to a church procession which was to pass by before very long. The procession was to be for the patron saint of the town.

He was finding out that in all of the buildings the upper floors contained beautifully furnished apartments, but the street floors were mediocre.

He was back in his room, which was on the second floor, and before very long the procession came by. He watched with the family from one of their balconies. About a block or two ahead of the procession, on its way to the church on the square, came the street sweepers. Leading the procession were girls dressed entirely in white, in two single columns on each side of the street. The smallest, about three years old, led the column, with the line graduating according to size up to girls of about eighteen. Spaced at intervals, in between the files of girls in white and veils, were older girls in white carrying church banners and the Italian flag.

Following the queues of girls came the monks dressed in their brown robes, which were tied with a cord similar to a bathrobe. Their heads were uncovered and each one had his head shaved, making a perfectly round bald spot. Following the monks in brown came the ones dressed in black, next the priests dressed with white surplices, next cerise, and finally the purple. With each color, there were fewer in number until there were only two who wore purple. Between the girls and the monks was a rather nondescript, but pleasant-sounding, band.

They had no order of march and more or less straggled along. Fred had seen the band many times. They were part of the church because they were usually with funerals. Following the priests came a religious statue upon an automobile decorated with flowers and made into a float. As the priests came by, people on the balconies tossed out rose petals. All along the street there was a continual shower of rose petals.

One thing, however, brought back the reality that this was a country at war. As the procession was going down the street, a convoy of trucks came up the street and had to break through the procession. With that one exception, there was nothing to mar the procession. Fred was sure that it would have been impossible to hold such a procession in northern Italy at that time because our planes were over them all the time.

There was a story in *Stars & Stripes* that really brought out the chuckles. An artillery spotter saw about eight or nine German soldiers going into a house. He thought that it must be a Headquarters of some sort, so he directed artillery fire upon the house. Shortly, the soldiers ran out, minus a considerable amount of their clothing, most of them in their underwear or less, followed by a group of signorinas in less than underwear.

Rome

July 1944

The Captain arrived in Rome one night about midnight and had quite a problem finding the Headquarters for which he was looking. He had the address but the problem was that the streets in Rome changed their names every few miles, something that he was not prepared to handle. Later, he found getting around Rome was really difficult. The streets went anywhere except into another street. Long streets would change their names every so often, which was most confusing and not amusing. However, he soon became able to find his way around. Rome was blacked out, of course, and trying to read the changing street names really made it hard to know where he was going. A bright moon helped quite a bit.

The Wing Headquarters got into Rome a few days after Rome was taken by the 5th Army. The Wing had stopped moving for awhile and was settled again.

In Rome it was certainly a pleasant sound to hear street cars running. Fred never thought the sound of street car wheels would be pleasant, but actually the first time he heard them, it was music to his ears.

The people in Rome were certainly different from those seen in the part of Italy just left. They were much cleaner, and the filth seen in the southern part of Italy was not in evidence. Although many of the people were poorly dressed, they were nevertheless clean. However, they were hungry. He took some laundry out, and the woman who did it did not want money at all. She did want something to eat, particularly for her bambino.

Many of the civilians looked as though there had never been a war, well dressed and good looking. The women must have had stocks of cosmetics available because rouge and lipstick were used by nearly all of them. Their clothes were up to date and of good material.

Fred talked to two American women, a real treat to once again be able to hear understandable communication from a woman. One of them left San Francisco in 1940 with her husband, arrived in Italy and could not go back. The other was married to an Italian and could not leave. He was stopped beside a curb, trying to obtain directions from an Italian. They saw him talking to the Italian and came up and asked whether they could help. It was the most welcome sound he had ever heard.

★ ★ ★

In his traveling around to the various units, Fred frequently would have a little extra time to look around either coming or going. Sometimes he would be through making his contacts at 1:00, so he just took from that time until supper time to get back.

★ ★ ★

Several of the officers went through St. Peter's on one of their days off. They were able to go up on the roof where the Dome began. There were shops up there, and they would have been able to go around and buy souvenirs except that the shops had been closed for some time. All around the edges were the statues of the apostles which could be seen from the street. The area was now closed entirely.

It was interesting to be on the highways that he had not been over before because there was so much evidence of the war. He saw towns that had been bombed all winter and were just a bunch of ruins. Convery went into many small towns and villages, many hardly recognizable as towns or villages, with not much more than the remains of walls. At the time, the smell was pretty bad from bodies that had not yet been buried. But he saw some beautiful places that were untouched by the war. The people were trying to return to their homes and recover anything they could. Farmers were digging around in what was left of their farms with the idea of building them up again. This was where the worst of the fighting took place. A few miles away would be a number of homes that had not been damaged at all.

All along the roads people were heading back. They all had two-wheel carts drawn by an ox, horse, or a cow. The carts were piled high with their belongings and nearly always there would be a papa, a mama, and the kids walking along the side. Then sometimes a truck would be piled in much the same manner but higher. None of them could put another piece of furniture anywhere. Also, there were innumerable people just walking back with a bag or a sack. Those people apparently did not have time to take anything with them, or maybe they thought it would be safe enough to leave their things behind.

General Barcus asked the Captain to make a trip with him up a high hill. To get there they took a winding road through a grove of trees. Apparently, some German soldiers had been left behind as snipers, and while on the way up, the General and Convery became their target. Bullets could be heard passing nearby with the usual zing. They both decided it was no place for them.

There had been quite a bit of fighting in the grove near Rome where Headquarters was camped. A lot of the trees had been shot up from artillery fire. Some were partially cut; others were down to the ground. Once when Lieutenant Hoffman was shaving, a slight breeze came up. Without any warning at all, the top of a tree came down beside him. Had he been hit he would have been badly hurt. A number of trees had been cut at the top and were lying at right angles on top of the other trees, not broken clear off.

★ ★ ★

Some of the meals at mess were not very good. For example, one dinner was string beans with pieces of leftover bacon and a poor grade of chili with red beans. Along with it there was bread, butter, lemonade, and canned pears. It does not sound too bad, and actually it wasn't, but the chili wasn't right, and lemonade on a cold, wet day just didn't make anyone happy.

One evening Fred invited Lieutenant Offing (who worked with him in the AA section), Lieutenant Harris (the officer who was married and worked in the A-3 section), and Lieutenant Hash (the statistician) to his tent for clam chowder. Esta furnished the minced clams of which he used three cans. He got an onion from the kitchen and swiped some bread and butter, as well as salt and pepper from the tables. A can of milk came from the kitchen, and one of the men walked off with a bottle of catsup. They made the chowder. It must have been good because they all raved over it. From the table they brought along some pieces of the bacon and the string beans. The clams, clam juice, bacon, pepper, and a little catsup really made a treat. For heat they used a small, single burner, portable Coleman-type gasoline stove. Toast was also made to go along with the chowder. Lieutenant Harris said Fred was a good enough cook for him to marry, if he were not already married.

★ ★ ★

Fred went to Army Headquarters and on the way back he had to make a side trip up into a mountainous area to a Battalion Headquarters. He went through a couple of towns that looked as though they had been there for centuries. The road wound around up a hill, and he passed through a cut just outside one of the small towns. All along the side were caves dug out of the soft rock. At first, he thought the caves were used by people to live in while they were getting out of the way of the war, which had passed by in the valley below. As he passed more of the caves, he realized they were being used by people to live in permanently. Each cave had either wooden double doors, which could be locked by a huge padlock, or a screen woven of dried briars. The briars were not movable as a door would be but were slanted inward with another wall of briar coming out from the opposite side, making an alley-way entrance. The briar was thick enough to prevent anyone from seeing in. Down on the lower part of the hill there were similar caves, which were under buildings. These were the stables for the livestock.

In June, Fred made a trip with a group of officers who were looking for radar sites in the hills. A situation developed in which Fred's limited Italian prevented a nasty development.

Because the front was moving fast, it was always necessary to find new radar sites. One location for which they were looking appeared to be excellent on the maps. They knew they were close to the lines but believed that the actual lines were quite a bit forward. It so happened that our troops had not gone through that particular section but had by-passed it. They were going along a narrow road, and a woman ran out very excited and said, "Tedesci, Tedesci," meaning "Germans." Fred talked to her, but she was not very sure how far up the road they were. They went a little farther on and met a man and a woman who had been walking along the road. The man told them that the Jerries were just over the next little hill. The group of officers consisted of a full colonel, a lieutenant colonel, two majors, three captains, and two lieutenants, in addition to the drivers. They were not up there as combat troops, so, needless to say, they did not go any farther. Fred was the only one there who could understand any Italian, and it was very limited. However, what he did know helped avoid confrontation with the Germans.

★ ★ ★

Some people were quite amiable and others did not want to

get acquainted at all. Handing out the hard candy that came with the C-rations helped make the people more friendly. Whenever any unit was on the move, C-rations were issued to the men before the move started. The C-rations came in individual cans. Each meal consisted of one can of hash or beans, a can of hard crackers, powder to make a drink of lemonade, coffee, or chocolate, and a couple of pieces of wrapped hard candy. The men did not always eat the candies, so they threw it out to the kids along the highways. There had not been any candy there for over two years. Candy was quite a treat.

★ ★ ★

Signal Battalion officers . . . Lt. Lonnie Temple on the left.

Lt. Lonnie Temple, who has been mentioned before, had charge of all of the wire communications to the radar sites and the airfields over the area under the 64th Fighter Wing command, which was Italy. Many times he would have lines run to the radar sites, and in doing so they would pass by AA sites, or close to various points at which the AA could make connections to any extra line that might be available. The first priority for all communications was the Fighter Wing Command. Occasionally, and quite frequently, the Signal Battalion would be activating and putting some damaged lines into service and would have a surplus of lines. These were the ones that would be made available to the AA units. This always entailed extra work on the Signal Battalion's part, and was not actually anything that was required of them to do.

★ ★ ★

This is where Convery came in. It might be called politics or whatever, but it was because he asked Lieutenant Temple to help out and get the lines to the guns that his section was able to get the information to the guns from the Control Room. This developed into quite a procedure that had never been used before. Its success was the reason that the high-ranking officers came to see what was being done. For one branch of the Armed Services to be performing services for another branch was anything but the norm. Of course, it had the approval of General Barcus.

Lonnie Temple was a person who loved his cigars. He was seldom seen without a cigar unless they were not available. Cigars were an item that was not issued with the supplies of cigarettes, candy, chewing gum, etc. and were very difficult to obtain. Along with Fred's requests to Esta for goodies, odds and ends, and canned things, etc., he asked her to send him cigars. She had to get them from under the counter at places around home and managed to locate enough for Fred to pass on to Temple. Fred never knew anyone quite as happy as Lonnie. He beamed when Fred had a cigar to pass along. Those cigars actually had a mighty big effect in the availability of wire communications to the AA, because whenever Temple would fix Fred's section up with a line to some unit, Fred would slip him a cigar, not a lot of them, just one or two. Actually, it was sort of bribery, but it certainly worked. Consequently, Esta should be given a considerable amount of praise and appreciation for her work in the war effort!!

In July, Captain Convery finally became settled into an assignment that was not temporary and was very desirable. Orders came through transferring him to the Wing. He was quite happy because the Wing Table of Organization listed the AA officer as a lieutenant colonel.

★ ★ ★

The various nationalities had their own nicknames. A British soldier was a *Limy*, the French were called *Goums*, but that mainly applied to the African French. When it came to fighting, the Goums were a tough and mean bunch. Any Italian was called a *Ginny*; most always they were referred to as *Goddamned Ginnies*. Our enlisted men were referred to as *GIs* (General Issue).

★ ★ ★

The Italian nights were truly beautiful, especially when there was a full moon. There was one on a night that they were showing movies to the troops. In 1944 there were short films along with a feature. With one of the movies, one of the shorts was most appropriate. It was one of those that led community singing. One of the songs was *By the Light of the Silvery Moon*.

It was rather amusing during the show because the words of the song were listed for boys and then for girls. Of course, there were no girls in the crowd but a number of the boys sang the girls' words in high falsetto soprano voices. The screen was set up on a bank and consisted of a sheet on a frame. There were quite a number of troops who came to see the movies. They sat on the hillside opposite the screen. The officers sat behind the screen as the picture showed through. It worked fine except that the titles had to be read backward and the actors were all left-handed and did everything toward the left, such as writing and shaking hands.

★ ★ ★

One time in July Fred got in at 12:15 a.m. after getting stuck on a road on the way home. The rear end of the jeep went out. In order to get back, they had to disconnect the drive shaft and come in using the front wheel drive. They couldn't just call up and have a garage send out help but did get some help from some boys on a seven-ton wrecker.

* * *

When it rained in Italy, it really rained. Fred, with his driver, was coming down a hill in the jeep, and it actually rained so hard that the coil got wet. When they stopped, the jeep wouldn't start, even going downhill. The only thing to do was to park it at the bottom of the hill, get under cover until the rain was over and do what they could do to dry off the coil. When they got back to the jeep, the spaces around the spark plugs were full of water and had to be dried out. When they stopped, he and his driver were soaked to the skin. Fred had his field jacket on, but the rain went right through that. When they got to the bottom of the hill, they saw a small house with a woman looking out the door, watching the rain come down, so they headed there to get out of the rain.

While they were waiting for the rain to quit, she told them that this was the place she and her family had come to live after their previous three places had been bombed. She and her husband had two daughters. Apparently, their previous home was a three-story house and quite nice.

This place was the size of a garage and had been used to store a tractor. The roof was made of corrugated iron, not altogether waterproof and, of course, was leaking. In this small area she had a double bed and a single bed. Both beds had nice bedspreads. In addition, there were several plain chairs and a dining table, quite nice, with a sideboard to match. She had to keep mopping up the water to keep it from spoiling the furniture. On the beds she had pans, not very many, to catch the water, and where she didn't have pans, she had rags. She showed Fred a radio which they had hid from the Germans. When the Germans came looking for whatever they wanted, they were told that they had nothing.

When the rain quit, the men went on their way. Another hour had to be spent drying out the jeep, still soaked, before they could start back. The sun came out and once they were riding in the jeep, they were dry in about an hour—that is except for their underwear.

That evening after supper Fred had to make a phone call back to where he had been that afternoon. While talking, the party there told him that it was raining to beat hell and had been for some time. He knew he was right because in about ten minutes it started in there. He tied up his tent and became quite snug. Some of the other tents were not staked down well enough, and with the strong wind they started to go. Many were running around wildly getting their tents restaked. It was thundering with lots of lightning all the time the rain was pouring down. He went out to help and got soaked again. Then he went back to his tent and put on dry clothing. He didn't put on clean clothes but fished out some dirty ones because he was not sure whether he would be out in the rain again before the night was over.

★ ★ ★

After the unit had moved into an area for a little while, livestock began to show up, having been hid from the Germans. Fred thought that either women or their clothing had been hidden also. They hardly ever saw a good-looking woman and those they did see wore very plain clothes. Where the clothes came from no one knew. But the women began showing up everywhere, well dressed in clean, nice-looking dresses. Makeup also began to make its appearance. The conclusion he drew was that they must have hidden their better clothes to keep them from being taken and didn't keep themselves too presentable in order to keep from being molested. After they found out that they wouldn't be bothered, they came out well dressed.

★ ★ ★

Lt. Shaw was the husband of a very good friend of Esta's. Fred had been trying to contact him by phone and finally made it. He was just down the road two or three miles from where Fred was at the time. His outfit had been there about a week. Fred

133

never expected to find him because he was usually around an airport. Shaw's unit was a quartermaster outfit that had just been bivouacked there and had been resting for a week. Fred went down to see him one afternoon and had a nice visit. It certainly seemed good to talk to someone he knew and to talk about people and places that were familiar to both. Shaw had not heard that his son was back from Italy, which Esta had written to Fred.

★ ★ ★

Fred had one especially interesting afternoon, as well as an evening. He didn't have a thing to do, so he took the jeep and just started driving to see what he could see. After wandering around awhile, he picked up what he thought were some sailors. They turned out to be three Navy officers who had some time off and were just out doing practically the same thing as Fred. They were not in proper uniform, which was the reason he did not recognize them as officers. They were tickled to death to be picked up and invited along. They did not have any transportation so it was hard for them to go places and see things. They usually would get into a port and about all they could see was what they could walk to and that was usually the poorer part of the town.

The group drove to some towns away from the main roads and up in the mountains. One place was an old monastery that was built on a high hill. To get to it, they had to follow a very poor and steep road. It was certainly not used by any type of vehicle except ox carts. It was so steep Fred had to put the jeep in its underdrive as well as its four-wheel drive. The turns were sharp and he had to back up at least once in order to get around them, and that was with a jeep. They all said if they hadn't seen it (the road and the jeep), they wouldn't have believed it. They got quite a kick out of it.

When they got to the monastery, they found a small settlement outside and around the building. One of the monks came out to see them. He spoke French, and because one of the Naval officers also spoke French, they were able to get along very well.

He showed them through the monastery and all through the garden. The garden had all kinds of vegetables, as well as a great variety of fruit trees. There were many different kinds of grapes for making varieties of wine. The men wanted to buy some, and the monk who was showing them around said that they could. But later on, after he had talked to his superior, they were told that they couldn't.

He told them that the monastery had been founded and built in the second century and had been modernized somewhat. They couldn't believe him and made him tell them three times because they thought they might have been mistaken. He said that the chapel was exactly as it had been built originally. Although small, it was certainly beautiful.

After they left the monastery, they drove to some other towns, just sightseeing and really enjoying themselves. In return for what had been done for them, they invited Fred to dinner aboard their ship, a destroyer berthed at Orbetello. For dinner they had some good steak and, believe it or not, a bottle of real American beer that was ice cold. It tasted good and was the first American beer Fred had had since he left the States. They visited the rest of the evening and then Fred went back to camp.

★ ★ ★

During the latter part of July, Captain Convery was sent into Naples to take part in the planning of the invasion of Southern France. His duty was to see to the coordinating and making of plans for the Early Warning Service to the AA Artillery taking part in the landing and invasion. Eight other officers and the Captain were billeted in an apartment house. They went to an officers' mess about a block away for their meals.

There were all kinds of training going on around the Naples harbor area and also other harbors nearby. Control Room personnel in small groups were working with Control Rooms to be set up on ships that were to be used in the invasion. Radars were placed on ships as widely apart as possible. Their information was to be passed to the Control Rooms aboard four different vessels. The number-one ship had the main Control Room and was the one that was to handle all Control Room matters until such time as it might become disabled. If the number-one ship became disabled, number-two would take over or number-three or four, whichever was necessary. The Control Room's primary mission was the handling of the fighter plane support cover for the invasion.

An AA officer and an enlisted man were scheduled to be with each ship and were to follow the same AA procedures as the normal functions of the regular Control Room. The plans provided that the AA officer in the Control Room aboard the number one-ship would begin transmitting information regarding hostile or friendly planes at the time of landing.

The plan was taken to the AA section of Army Headquarters. They then put the orders out to all of the AA units that were scheduled to go in with the invasion. The units were advised that, immediately upon arriving on the beach and getting their guns set up, they should tune in on the frequency that was assigned to the Anti-Aircraft force for broadcasting to the AA artillery only. In this manner, there would be information available as soon as the guns became functional. The broadcasts were to be in the clear.

General Kelly, the AA General of Army Headquarters, agreed to the plan and thought that it would work in good shape. However, he wanted to have the whole program set up as an Army procedure. Captain Convery advised him of all the equipment that was entering into the program through the Air Force and of how the AA was having the use of it by the placing of four officers, one on each ship, with the one enlisted man. He approved. He knew that the Army did not have either the equipment or the personnel to do the job. No other invasions or landings had had this set up of Early Warning for the AA Artillery.

For several days, probably a week, the fighter bombers of the Wing were given missions to bomb a beach along the coast of the

Mediterranean up near the Italian border, someplace in the neighborhood of Nice. A considerable number of Sorties were made to that point. There were no plans whatsoever to make a landing there, but the idea was to give the Germans the feeling that this was where we were going to land. The beach that was to be used for the invasion was around Toulon and St. Raphael. The ship that Convery was going to be on was scheduled to land everybody at St. Tropez, a summer resort.

Prior to the landing, our reconnaissance planes flew all along the coast and took pictures of the entire coastline of Southern France. That made it possible to know what the area was going to look like upon landing. The AA Headquarters had decided on a certain road near St. Tropez to set up their Headquarters in a stone quarry. The planning of the invasion lasted several weeks.

★ ★ ★

One evening just before supper Lieutenant Colonel Romenan and Fred were standing on the balcony of the rooms in which they were quartered, having a "bull session." Romenan was a lawyer from Oklahoma and had been around cattle quite a bit. They were talking of branding, roping, breaking horses, etc. Fred told him of the experience Esta had with the dead calf that was still in the cow. They swapped similar situations and how sometimes the calf would have to be turned over, or have its feet placed right, before the calf could be dropped.

Some Italian women were on the balcony above them but the two men did not pay any attention to them because they were talking in Italian. Pretty soon, one of the women shook out a rug over their heads, and as Fred looked up, she said, "Excuse me." On the way back from supper, it occurred to Fred that they had been talking a little rough, and because she had said "Excuse me," he knew that she was able to speak and understand English. So Fred went up to the rooms above to apologize to her. A gray-haired lady, who must have weighed 200 pounds, came to the door. He asked, in the best way he could, for the lady who spoke

English. She explained that her daughter (he saw her again on the balcony and she must have been at least fifty) was in bed. He told her that he would return later.

The next day he went up to apologize and what an experience he had. The mother came to the door, saw Fred, and said something in Italian. Her husband then came. He was little, dried up and had a Hindenburg-type mustache and spoke English. He was mad as anyone could be, because Fred had the nerve to speak or even ask to speak to his daughter. He was the one to see if Fred wanted to talk to anyone there. Fred got rather mad himself and told him *to go plumb to hell.* That was one of the reasons some of the Italians were called "Goddamn Ginnies!"

The Americans got fed up with some of the Italians, especially those who had lived among the U.S. troops for a while. At first the Italians were respectful, and then they seemed to think that we were serving them and that they could tell us what to do and when to do it. The Germans had the right idea to some extent, which was to kick them around a bit and they would respect you for it. But treat them nice and decent and they thought you were groveling.

Fred had tough luck with his cuisine for few days. Chicken was issued all through the area and every mess had a chicken dinner over the weekend. But he ate at three different messes, missing the chicken dinner every time. Not only that, but the meals he had were poor. That's the way it went though. Whenever a good meal came along, the ration schedule was balanced off with a bum one, and he hit all of the bad ones.

Newspaper clipping from *Stars & Stripes Weekly:*
"AT A FORWARD AIRBASE"
There are a couple of Messerschmitt pilots now learning to play harps who wish they'd learned about the new American Mustang. There are also a couple of

twenty-year-old American pilots who will tell you this latest-model Mustang is the grandest job wearing wings.

The Messerschmitt pilots are dead. The Americans are back in the air looking for fresh meat. And thereon hangs a tale of day-by-day air action in the 1st Tactical Air Force directed by Maj. Gen. John K. Cannon.

Strictly speaking, 1st Lt. William R. Hornsby, Tampa, Florida, and 2nd Lt. Warner E. Johnson, Bozeman, Montana, aren't supposed to be shooting Kraut planes. Their job, as it was at Sicily and Salerno, is reconnaissance. They go out on daily patrol to spot enemy gun positions, troop concentration traffic and so on.

On this particular day, however, they were jumped by two ME-109s around 4,000 feet. The site was the Tiber River. The German pilots thought they had a couple of soft touches, and didn't realize their mistake until they were practically on top of the Mustangs.

The MEs hit for the dirt and started hedge-hopping for a safe port. Hornsby and Johnson went after them. Johnson, in particular, was out for blood. He and a pal had been jumped by 12 MEs on their fourth mission. The memory lingered on.

"My man was easy," said Johnson. "In fact, I caught him so fast I had to put down the flaps to keep from overrunning him. I gave him a burst from about 20 yards and saw the pilot slump. The plane crashed a moment later."

Hornsby's story was much the same.

"I had to kick the rudder hard to miss Jerry. He was moving fast, but he might as well have been anchored. I gave him 60 rounds, and he exploded."

★ ★ ★

In August, papers were being prepared to be sent in for the promotion of Captain Convery to major. He did not know if they would go through because there was a regulation that the officer must be in the vacancy for at least three months, and he had only been assigned to the Wing since June 27. A statement was going along with the recommendation explaining that he performed the work for the Wing while on TD (Temporary Duty).

Convery was a little hasty in writing about that recommendation for a *Major*. It had started all right, but a telegram came through that all promotions had been held up until further notice.

However, he cleaned his summer, tropical, worsted pants and shirt in 100 octane gas. One of the officers brought some in from one of the airstrips. That stuff certainly did a good job of cleaning.

A few days later Convery again had news about the promotion. Captain Butler, the Adjutant, told him that the order that had come through for recommendations for promotions had been unfrozen.

★ ★ ★

A story was going around about a war correspondent who sneaked into Rome by a back road before the Germans had left. He had been on the go for a number of days and was dead tired. He got to a hotel without being noticed—the Germans were not paying much attention to anyone—and was given a room. There he found a German officer packing. The officer asked to be given about five minutes and said he would be out. Then the correspondent had a good meal with a bottle of wine, a bath, and went to bed intending to sleep around the clock. He was awakened the next morning by feeling something cold on his face. He opened his eyes and found himself looking into the muzzle of the biggest gun he had ever seen and someone saying, "Get out, you lazy Kraut, so we can get in." He asked who in the hell they were and was told that they were correspondents. They even gave names of their papers. He replied, "I'm so and so of————Times. Get out yourself and let me sleep!" I don't suppose they did, but the chain of circumstances was rather funny.

★ ★ ★

Fred broke in a new pair of shoes. They were the regular Army shoes—heavy, thick, leather soles that resembled and felt like boards. The rough side of the leather was on the outside. An extra piece of leather was sewn to the tops and fastened with a buckle. They were known as combat boots. He put them on, and into each one poured a tumbler of water. He wore them from the afternoon until about bedtime. The leather became soft and shaped to his foot. The extra piece of leather made it unnecessary to wear leggings, which was the main reason for the leather. Shaping the soles to his feet made them as comfortable as a pair of old slippers.

★ ★ ★

Convery went to the PX with Captain Butler, and Butler asked whether he had any *major's leaves*. He told him no, and he certainly did not intend to buy any ahead of time. That would be the worst kind of bad luck.

★ ★ ★

Fred went out to dinner with Captain Butler to the home of some friends of Butler's whom he had known for a long period of time. He really felt that he would burst before he got through. The food was not fancy but well cooked, and each dish was served as a separate course. The Italians really only ate two meals a day—one about 1:30 in the afternoon and the other about 9:00 or 9:30 at night. The first meal was not very heavy so that when dinner came around they really went to town. The Italians felt hurt if their guests did not do the same. The dinner started out with olives and cold ham; next a big bowl of spaghetti (which was a meal by itself); a plate of French-fried potatoes; slices of roast beef; a plate of salad; big ears of fresh corn; bread with each course; with beer and wine to drink. They kept filling his glass whenever he took a drink. For dessert they had watermelon. The Italians were really artists at serving food. The hostess, rather than the host, always served everything after it had been brought in by a maid. When the hostess served the melon, she cut it by making round slices about two inches thick. Then she cut those in half and cut the meat away from the rind, which was a rather nice way of serving melon.

PART IV

FRANCE

Landing at St. Tropez August 1944

About ten days were spent in loading aboard the freighters for the invasion of Southern France. Each individual could only take along the personal supplies that could be carried on his back. Everything else was packed for following shipment.

The convoy left the Naples area, and passed between Corsica and Sardinia, heading for Southern France. It arrived off the shores of St. Tropez around midnight and lay there without any movement at all. Orders were to be absolutely quiet because they were not too far away from shore, and noises would be carried across the water. It was a still night. There was no wind or air movement of any kind. No one did much sleeping. The first attack was to be just before daylight. Everyone was very tense.

★ ★ ★

The following excerpt is from "*History of the 64th Fighter Wing*":

> In the dawnlight of 15 August 1944 bombardments were fiercely under way. H-Hour would be 0800. Behind the first invasion fleet the heavy guns of the battleships flashed in the half-light and sent their projectiles screaming into the enemy shore defenses and coastal gun positions. Above the beaches Tac/R aircraft

directed the bombardment and called over the VHF when they spotted an enemy gun flash. Closer to the beaches destroyers and light cruisers fired smaller guns into lesser enemy gun positions, field artillery positions and anything which might endanger the lives of Allied troops when they rushed ashore.

Following their attacks of the previous night, heavy bombers swept over the beaches at seven o'clock and bombed continually for a half hour through the ground haze and overcast. Fighter-bombers and mediums flashed in during the last moments before the troops came ashore. Their 1000 pound and 500 pound demolition and general purpose bombs hurtled downward, exploding among the ack-ack positions, coastal defenses, troop concentrations and field artillery emplacements. Lighter bombs were dropped on the beaches to make paths for the ground troops through the barbed wire entanglements.

This was invasion. The technique developed on previous invasions was applied skillfully, and the overwhelming superiority of every force held by the Allies was used against the entrenched enemy. For many of the men participating, this was the fourth and last invasion they would make in Europe.

★ ★ ★

The day before the landing didn't seem to be any different than any other day aboard ship except that everyone had to wear a helmet when on deck. That was all right, but, in addition, they had to go below whenever there was an alert. Below deck was much safer than above because the deck of the ship consisted of four inches of steel—rather a satisfying feeling.

The officers all stayed together on a sort of sub-bridge, just below the Captain's bridge. It was a good place to see everything going on. Only a small part of all of the ships could be seen, but even so it was quite impressive. There was a feeling of being strong and powerful. Seeing the troop ships in columns with battleships and destroyers was a sight not to be forgotten. There were no words to describe the mixture of emotions. It was a strong force, as strong as possible. With the combination of every kind of warship, all types of planes ready to go to work when needed, and planning to the last detail, it didn't seem possible that the invasion could fail. Yet, there was the unknown shore of Southern France which was being approached.

Even though land could not be seen and would not be seen until the following dawn, everyone on deck, except those reading or playing games, continually watched the horizon ahead, wondering what it held for him personally.

The ship was packed with men and officers, but was not as packed as some of the ships accompanying. Most of them had landing boats hung all along the sides similar to lifeboats. Knowing that those landing boats would be used in the assault, one could not help but wonder how they would make out and whether any of them would contain anyone known.

Three meals were given the day before D-Day, which was out of the regular order of things because the regular schedule was only two meals a day.

From the time the convoy left port, everyone had to wear a life preserver at all times except while sleeping, and then it had to be handy. Before leaving, Fred was able to get a May West. That's a type of life preserver used by pilots and is not nearly as bulky as the kapok type. It was made of rubber and was worn like a bib or an apron. The head went through an opening. One strap went around the back and fastened on the opposite side. Another strap ran from the center in front, between the legs and looped so that the strap going around the back went through the loop of the strap going between the legs. It was made in two sections, one on top of the other, which were inflated separately. Each section had a small metal cartridge of compressed air, which was released by pulling a string. If you had to jump from a ship, you never released the compressed air until you were in the water. With the May West full of air, it would hit you on the chin when you hit the water, knocking you out. The May West was painted a bright yellow so that anyone in the water could be easily seen. By the way, the reason it was called a May West was because of the buxom appearance it gave when inflated.

★ ★ ★

The following note was given out to everybody shortly after leaving the port of Naples:

> Soldiers of the Seventh Army, we are embarking for a decisive campaign in Europe. Side by side, wearing the same uniform and using the same equipment, battle-experienced French and American Soldiers are fighting with a single purpose and common aim—destruction of Nazism and the Germans. The agonized people of Europe anxiously await our coming. We cannot and will not fail. We will not stop until the last vestige of German tyranny has been completely crushed. No greater honor could come to us than this opportunity to fight to the bitter end in order to restore all that is good and decent and righteous in mankind. We are an inspired Nation. God be with us.

★ ★ ★

The following is a letter Fred sent home to his wife Esta:

> August 14, 1944
> (Mailed August 18)
> Aboard Ship
> I don't know when I will have a chance to mail this letter or, as far as that is concerned, if I will even have a chance. When I mail it, my address will be "Somewhere in France." When we will be able to say we are in France is something I don't know now. But, of course, we will be able to someday, and when the day

comes, I will send this on to you.

Because of my assignment, I had to be in on the plans for a long time. I was really worried that I might let something slip. We have been aboard ship for almost a week, and although we have been comfortable, a troop ship is rather boring.

There is no place to sit on the deck unless we actually sit down on the deck, so we stand up all the time while we are topside. We have a stateroom and, of course, spend a lot of time there. In ours, there are 12 officers, all captains. The bunks are stacked three high with four tiers, two on a side. These would be quite comfortable if it were not for the heat. The air is fresh enough and changes rapidly, but it is awfully hot. There is so much heat combined with moisture that we perspire continuously even though we are lying still. I was reading in my bunk yesterday, and I had to keep my mouth closed to keep the sweat from running in. I drink a lot of water which accounts for most of it.

In our room, we have a French liaison officer who is quite interesting. He speaks very good English. He was in the French Army at the time of the fall of France, was a prisoner for nine months, and then escaped to Africa, fighting through Africa and then through Italy. All the while, he has been looking forward to this event we are now on.

A short time after we land, he expects to see his aunt and a little later his five-year-old son whom he has not seen for four years. Yesterday we were able to buy PX supplies, and he purchased several boxes of hard candy and a carton of Life Savers to take to his son. There has been no sugar or candy in France, so this should be quite a treat for his son.

Although I have known the general plans for some

time, we received more detailed plans last night. From what I have been able to gather, the operation should be a success.

We have to depart the ship by noon tomorrow, which will be within eight hours of the first wave. I have a peculiar feeling. I don't know whether to be scared or not, yet I know I should be. I don't seem to be worried about getting hurt or injured because I have that feeling I have had so many times before, "I'll come out all right." The thing I am worried about is whether I will be able to get back to you. That seems to be the big worry in my mind. That probably doesn't make sense, but nevertheless that is how it is. I'll know the answer to-morrow. Anyway, we are heading home.

Before long the big guns of the battleships opened up. One could hear but could not see the firing on the beach. Pretty soon the mists lifted, and the beach could be seen. By that time, the attack had advanced inland, and from time to time word came back about how it was going. We left the ship about the middle of the afternoon going down the sides of the ship by landing net. It so happened that the boat hit the beach at a place where we could step right onto the shore, Actually, I was disappointed in the landing because the boat was able to pull right up to the beach. I went up over the bow and jumped off onto dry sand. I did not even get the soles of my feet wet. The boat next to ours was not so lucky, and the men from that one had to wade ashore with the water up to their shoulders. Altogether it was quite a show, not to be missed for anything, but it was nothing that anyone would pay an admission to see.

★ ★ ★

The following is another letter sent home to Esta from somewhere in Southern France:

I brought a candle along but that was soon used up

because everyone did not bring one. We could only bring along what we could carry ourselves on our backs, and not knowing what was ahead, I packed as light as I could. I am still living with the stuff I carried on my back when we came ashore because the rest of it has not caught up yet. It has been almost two weeks since I saw my stuff, and it will probably be another ten days to two weeks before it catches up. Jerry has not been very bothersome, although he has done some damage, enough to keep us worried.

On the morning we took off, we were up at 3:00 a.m. for breakfast, and of course everyone got his gear ready. By this time, a lot of us were worrying about carrying our load. Mine was not too heavy, and I knew that I could carry it all. But many were worrying about where they could put some things so that, if necessary, they could drop something and still have what they needed. They also saw the landing nets over the side of the ship and were wondering how they could carry it all down. In order to waterproof the rifle muzzles, wallets, watches, etc., a lot of rubber condoms began showing up. Fastened over the muzzle end of rifles, they were excellent. They also stretched over a billfold. I had three, which had been issued to me in Africa, so I put one over my watch, but the one over my billfold split. I tried the last one but it split also. So I tried to borrow a fresh one, but by that time they were all gone so I was out of luck. By the time we were ready to leave the ship, the one on my watch split, so I put my watch, pistol, and wallet in my field bag, which was the highest point on me and would be the last to get wet.

Getting back to the story, we were not allowed on deck until 5:15, and then the time was changed to 6:00. Some went back to sleep, but I couldn't. I went on deck and found the sea as quiet as a mill pond, with the mist so heavy that I could not see much beyond the next ship. The ship next to us with the landing boats had some already in the water. We had no idea where we were but we had some idea that we were off the southern coast of France. We knew Jerry did not know we were there because he had not opened up yet. It was really a dramatic time. I had an eerie feeling, and others were talking in hushed voices as they tried to look through the mists toward the shore, wondering what was there. I was standing beside a young soldier, and we were both looking over the railing down toward the water. As an example of how nervous everyone was, he said, "The tide is sure high tonight." High tide or low tide, the distance from the railing down to the water would be the same.

Upon landing on the beach, a place was found on shore to be comfortable and they got themselves organized. After they reached their assembly point, they got adjusted, taking several hours. The pine grove they were in resembled a busy picnic ground that had been the scene of a number of platonic friendships—play for him and tonic for her. Finally getting settled, Fred acquired a jeep and driver and started to look for the AA Headquarters which was supposed to be in a stone quarry. He had to go through a small town and came to a three-story building surrounded by troops keeping cover and advising everyone else to do the same. A number of snipers were holed up in the building, and he could not get through with the jeep until the snipers had been cleaned out.

In looking for the stone quarry, Fred drove for several hours on whatever roads could be found leading north, because the quarry was supposed to be located on a north-south road to the east about one mile. It became dark, and he was still looking for

AA Headquarters on those strange roads. With no lights and a dark night, it was really difficult. He had no map of the area and had no idea exactly where he was. He followed a good road going north and thought that it might be off of that road. He asked many GIs whether they had seen anything of the quarry, and none of them had. They headed north for quite a distance, and a GI told them there was a command post a short distance away. He went to the command post to see whether he could get any information about the quarry. They knew nothing about it, but he did find out that this command post was the farthest point of the day's advance and that it was thought the Germans were up the road a short distance. Discretion being the better part of valor, he started back.

On the way back down the road, he saw a beer truck turned on its side in the ditch beside the road. It had been on the road at the time the invasion started early in the morning and the driver had left his truck there and taken off for the hills. By that time, it was about 10:30 p.m.

Fred finally got back to the assembly point and told one of the sergeants what he had seen on the road and just exactly where the truck was. He asked what Fred wanted him to do. He said "nothing" and that he was just reporting the situation. The sergeant asked to borrow Fred's jeep. Later on that night Fred was invited to have a bottle of beer from a pile of a half dozen cases that had somehow appeared in the area. Needless to say, by morning all that was left were empty cases.

St. Raphael

Six days after landing they had power for the first time. The power was not from their own power plant, because the power plants had not yet caught up with them. Jerry left in such a hurry that he was not able to sabotage the power plants. Headquarters was established in a beautiful old French chateau that was originally built in the 1600s and remodeled about 1890.

One of the troubles during the first few days was snipers who had been left behind. Needless to say, they were dealt with rather harshly when they were located.

On one of Fred's trips, while looking for a location to set up a Headquarters, he was with two other officers and a driver in a jeep. They were going up a road and began hearing bullets passing by quite close. They got out of there and tried to find out where the shooting was coming from. It was discovered that there was a sniper located in the attic of a house, shooting through a hole in the roof that had been made by the removal of a tile. It was not long before he was located and became a casualty.

The people in France were different from those in Italy. Of course, in France we really were liberators, whereas in Italy we were only liberators to those who were not Fascists. The people in Italy were not pretending to like us, but in France we felt we had real friendship. They really smiled at us, and almost all of them waved as we passed. After the troops were in a town for awhile, they didn't wave quite as much, but when they did they all held up their hands in a V.

Twice the Captain was in towns just after they had been cleared. Once when Colonel Nelson and the Captain were going through a town and asked an MP about the situation ahead, he told them that the town had been taken the night before by the tanks and that the infantry had gone in that morning after figuring that everything was okay. They noticed that the place had not been cleaned of debris, etc. There was a considerable amount of equipment lying around and a number of German vehicles. There were also quite a number of dead still about. The Colonel spoke very good French, and he asked how long it had been since the fighting had stopped. They learned most of the snipers had just been cleared out about twenty minutes before.

However, some German snipers were left behind while our tanks and infantry went through. Then when there were not many soldiers around, the snipers went to work again. However, the partisans took care of them, and they didn't take many prisoners.

When going through one of the small towns, the people were all out on the sidewalks, waving them through. Of course, they waved back to them. One time while going along quite close to a curb, somebody was waving or holding out his hand to shake hands, and as their hands touched he grabbed hard and hung on. The Captain's arm went back against the jeep's side, and he thought that it would break before the civilian let loose.

★ ★ ★

The invasion advance wave was up the Rhone Valley. Convery had to make a trip the day following an attack on a retreating German division on the main road. Most of the division was destroyed. Apparently, the whole column had been trapped on the road by our planes, fighter planes and dive bombers—mostly dive bombers. Many of the vehicles had tried to get off the road and into the fields but got stuck in the plowed fields. They were then destroyed by the planes. It was surprising to see many, many horse-drawn vehicles. Every kind of a vehicle was being used by the Germans and pulled by horses. Apparently, the German Army had decided to send most of the motorized equipment to the other front and was using mainly horse-drawn equipment. In destroying the equipment, the planes would also kill the horses as well as many of the German personnel. The dead horses had begun to bloat.

When the Wing Headquarters landed at St. Tropez and took over a French chateau, some paratroopers came by and stopped with them for awhile. They told how bitter they were about some of the planes that had taken part in the invasion and had carried paratroopers. The planes, when carrying the paratroopers and flying at night, had no visual idea where they were and had to depend on radar information regarding where and when the paratroopers could be dropped. Apparently some mistakes were made and paratroopers were dropped during the middle of the night into the Mediterranean rather than on land. When that happened, there was no hope whatsoever for the paratrooper because he was loaded with all kinds of heavy equipment as well as ammunition, hand grenades, etc. When the paratrooper hit the water, there was nothing, absolutely nothing, to keep him from going straight to the bottom. It was the one thing that they feared more than anything.

Captain Butler came to see Fred for information regarding his promotion. It could not be submitted just before they left Italy because the forms were not available. They had been packed. Fred gave him all he needed from memory except the order number and paragraph number making him a captain. Butler would have to wait until the files caught up with the outfit. The files were in a truck somewhere.

Fred came back from a long trip throughout the newly-captured areas. He was pooped—no foolin'. The trip seemed to be much harder than usual. The distance was not much more than other days, but he rode in a fixed-up jeep. He thought at one time that it would be a smart idea to put in a different seat. The seat was a good one, having been taken out of a passenger car. It had good springs, red leather, and chrome pipe work, but the angle was not right. His back was about to break in two. The road was over some mountains, and, although the road was good macadam, it was very winding. On the way up he was caught behind a long convoy that took forever to get around. He planned to be back at least by 2:00 in the afternoon, but it was after 6:00 when he got in.

He had to make a trip to what was called at that time a Chick Sales Specialty (an outdoor toilet). The boys built the seat too high and feet could not touch the ground. In the morning no one held up the parade because if anyone stayed too long their legs would go to sleep.

★ ★ ★

One experience made Fred feel mighty sorry for a sailor. Two sailors had some time off and started to see part of the country. They came to an area that was full of barbed wire and signs all over saying *Achtung-Minen* (Attention: Mines). But they went along through a patch anyway and started to walk along the beach. Of course, the obvious happened. One of them stepped on a mine, and it blew his left foot off. His friend ran all the way up to the medical officer, who left with an ambulance to take care of the boy. If people had been more careful, so many of those things would not have happened.

★ ★ ★

Esta wrote and said that she tried to buy a slice of ham. She was told that there wasn't any because it was all going to the Armed Forces. Maybe it was, but it was not getting into France. Ham was seen only once or twice since arriving in Africa in May of 1943. They did have bacon but no ham. Maybe the ham was going into that luncheon meat called Spam, but that definitely was not ham. No doubt it was being used in the States.

★ ★ ★

Things seemed to be breaking wide open. In two weeks time, almost as much territory had been taken in Southern France as was taken in Northern France in three months. That was not a result of stronger attack but of weaker defenses.

Sometime in September Fred had to make a trip that took three days. He covered over 600 miles, 300 the first day, a little driving the second day, and 275 the third. The trip was a loop of the entire area which was almost all of the area that had been taken. He passed through St. Raphael, LeLuc, Aix, Aigon, Montelimar, Vallence, Voiron, Grenoble, Fiesteron, St. Tropez, and a number of other small towns.

Another trip took him through beautiful country. He went through the lowlands one way and the mountains coming back. He could understand why the French loved their France. The French Alps were positively beautiful. Probably it was the valleys that made the Alps so pretty. They were green and well cultivated. The mountains were like the ranges around Mt. Rainier. They were not snow covered at that time of the year. All through the valleys were houses with red tile roofs. Sometimes the roofs would be a dark brown, a result of a light covering of moss. Being in cottons, Fred nearly froze to death, along with his driver.

In one area, Kaiserlauten, he passed through where another division of the German Army had been trapped in a mountain pass. Never had he seen so much destroyed equipment. They had been trying to get across a river to escape but couldn't. For about 25 miles, there were cars or trucks, one right after the other, burned up, guns of every description, and all kinds of personal equipment. Hundreds of dead horses had been there for three days, and many of them had not been buried or burned and the stench was terrific. The horses were bloated and their intestines were coming out. All of the people on the highway had handkerchiefs tied over their noses. There were probably a number of German soldiers there also but none could be seen.

Fred went through one fairly large town that had just been taken the day before, and the people were celebrating. Included in the celebration was a parade of the girls who favored the Germans. As was the custom, their heads were shaved and a swastika was painted on their bellies. The girls were all stripped naked.

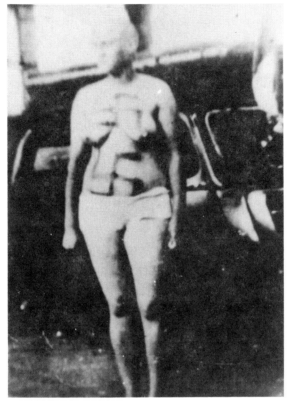

Naked girl with swastika

All along the streets and crossroads people were waving. There were many along the highway. They came from everywhere. There would be houses and no crossroads, but the people would be there. Old and young would be out, mothers holding their babies and waving the babies' hands, and toddlers just holding their hands up because they wanted to do as everyone else was doing. Some of the youngsters had their dolls along and were waving the arms of the dolls. Some could not wave enough with one hand, so they would wave both and jump up and down at the same time.

All held their fingers in the spread V. Everybody remarked that they had never seen so many good-looking women. Everybody wondered about that and believed the reason they saw so many was that they were dressed up in their Sunday best, plus they were all smiling. Fred looked at some while they were busy looking at something else, and they were actually no different than women at home or anywhere else, but their smiles made them good looking.

★ ★ ★

Newspaper clipping from *Stars & Stripes Weekly:*
"LETTER BY CAPTURED GERMAN DESCRIBES RHONE VALLEY ROUTE"

From a mammoth garage used by German ordinance men in Besancon before the Americans moved in, a German soldier sat down on Sept. 4 to write a letter home. When he was captured, the letter was found on his person. It describes the route of the German Army from Southern France up the Rhone Valley as it looked to a soldier in retreat. The "motor pool" he describes in the letter was since taken over by American ordinance men, who had more time and tools to put in action the vehicles the Germans left behind.

★ ★ ★

Besancon 4 Sept. 1944
Dear Mrs. Borchert:

Ever since 21 August we've been on the run and today we have landed in Besancon, where we're working in the motor pool trying to get some vehicles going. So far, thank God, I've survived. Everything was at stake. When seeing the picture along the route of withdrawal on the right bank of the Rhone, one couldn't help but think of the passage in the Bible where it said that the Lord punished them, men, horses, wagons and all.

There they were on foot, on stolen bicycles, on horses and all imaginable kinds of vehicles, three abreast. What a jam that was! Because of the dive bombers we could only ride at night; during the day we crawled into some hole under cover. In the daytime we can't travel more than 15-25 miles but at night we drive 10 hours. The roads in front of us have to be cleared of terrorists (he refers, probably, to the FFI) so that once we had to wait for two days before being able to continue. Once we tried to take off at 1900 hours and received a thorough peppering from dive bombers, resulting in two hits on our own vehicles.

As soon as airplanes approach, no matter at what distance, vehicles are abandoned and everybody disappears as fast as their legs will take them. There are long columns of vehicles slowly burning out. Horses fall on top of the other. Unfortunately they can not take cover, so they are being mowed down. We feel like chased rabbits and the Americans apparently get a big kick out of it, especially since we have no defense at all.

Large convoys were completely destroyed. The men must continue on foot, so everyone hikes along, with a stick in his hand and a bread sack as the only baggage. The road is littered with articles of equipment and arms. We, too, threw everything away, all furniture, coats, shoes, underwear, and all records and files. The only thing we kept were three typewriters; not a piece of paper, not a single form... Now it's only 200 kilometers to Germany, but that, too, is an area thick with terrorists, and the dive bombers are still around. Let's hope we can still get through. Now the Americans have taken Lyons, too.

Pages could be written about this flight. It looked horrible in the towns through which we passed. Everything pillaged, everything torn out of the drawers, everything stolen by the Landsers. Wine especially was spilled in large quantities. And here everything is at an end. First of all the nice weather—it rains and is as cold as can be. Sleeping in the open is out. At night we practically freeze to death. Wine is expensive and hard to get. No more fruit can be bought either, due to transport difficulties from the south. (And here the letter ends.)

★ ★ ★

Another officer and Fred were making a trip during the first part of September and had to stop overnight at a small inn. While the innkeeper was fixing Fred a drink of homemade French whiskey, which was like nothing else under the sun and strong enough to be the sun, he told him that he learned to speak English while he was cooking at the Savoy in London. That seemed to be true because his meal was excellent. Where he got the meat was not known, but his steaks were the best since Fred left Los Angeles. He made a soup that was all right because it tasted good, but no one had the faintest idea what it was.

The innkeeper said that the waitress was his daughter, a pretty girl of about 22. He also said that she had a two-month-old baby who was in the vicinity of Bordeaux, but she did not know where or who it was with. No questions were asked, but maybe she was one of the girls the Germans had bred. If such was the case, she had been picked because she was such a pretty girl.

About that time the lights went out, and all were given candles. The four went upstairs to bed—Captain Sikes, the two drivers, and Fred—by the light of a candle apiece. When they were about halfway up the open stairs, the daughter burst out laughing. They asked a Norwegian lady why she was laughing. She replied that they looked exactly like four little girls going to bed at a convent. Apparently, she must have been raised in a convent, perhaps while her father was cooking at the Savoy. They had a good sleep and got up early to start out through the mountains, nearly freezing to death in the process.

One night Fred was settled and quite comfortable in his tent. He had hung onto the kerosene stove he got from his British friends in Africa and had the luxury of a warm tent. There were not any stoves at all, and because the weather was damp and cold, he was quite the envy of everyone. He tried not to have too much stuff to carry, just the essentials and a few things to make life comfortable. He was taught that a good soldier kept himself warm, dry and healthy. The soldier who said "I can take it" and tried to live unnecessarily in miserable conditions soon became sick and a problem.

★ ★ ★

Headquarters had quite a day in camp. A couple of officers who spoke French arranged for a gathering, or picnic, for the people at a nearby town. The word must have spread over miles and miles, because they came from everywhere to see the Americans. None were expected to be in the camp because the celebration was supposed to be down in the town. But all afternoon they came into our camp to look us over. The situation got a little out of hand. The General did not like to have so many people around the camp. Fred did not go down to the town because there was a Major and a Captain coming to see him and he had to stick around. A lot of the people came with eggs as presents. Fred exchanged presents, giving them candy. Captain Butler came in and they made coffee and had some of the eggs.

★ ★ ★

Excellent maps were provided of France. At the beginning of the war, the Army had obtained plates of all the maps put out by the Michelin Tire Co., who had maps in the same manner as Standard, Union, and other oil companies did in the States, with very good detail. Of course, all of the towns' names and other pertinent information within the maps was in French. However, on the margins was all of the information necessary to follow the maps, including explanations of the legends written in English. Consequently, all units got along fine. Those maps were absolutely invaluable.

* * *

On a trip when going into the city of Dole, it seemed very modern. Street cars were running, and there was quite a bit of traffic. People were crowding the streets as though there never had been a war. The buildings were not damaged and several destroyed bridges across the river were the only evidence of the war. One of the bridges had been repaired by building a temporary single-lane span, which could not handle the traffic the bridges had formerly handled. Nearly all of the trucks and cars (civilian) used charcoal for fuel. We got used to seeing them, but at first it looked funny to see cars and trucks going down the road with a couple of furnaces fastened onto the back of the car. The furnaces looked a good deal like hot water tanks without insulation. The attachment worked on any car and it came in all sizes. A sackful of charcoal would run a passenger car about 60 or 70 miles. The power was not as good as gasoline but it got them there. Absolutely no gasoline was available.

Truck with charcoal burner

In two days Fred and his driver covered about 450 miles. That was quite a bit considering that time had to be taken out for making contacts and taking care of his work of advising AA units where they could make connections with a line from the Operations Room.

They did not get started until about 10:00 in the morning, which made them late all the way through. Although roads were generally good, they were slowed by the bridges and culverts that were out. Sometimes it was quite a job to make sure they were on the right road. He had to work closely with the road map, and unless they were absolutely sure of where they were all the time, it was easy to get off the route.

The one thing complicating travel in a strange country with a different language is that sometimes they would come to an intersection or crossroads with several turns or maybe be in a town that had unmarked streets. In those cases, questions had to be asked, and the French pronunciation of the names of towns, streets, and roads was nothing like the spelling on the maps. Jerry also took a lot of road signs down and painted some out, all of which further confused everyone.

Heading for one town on their first day out, Fred and his driver found when they got there that a bridge had been blown, dividing the town. To get to the other side, it was necessary to drive about 75 miles—that is, a total of 75 miles, going to the next town, where a temporary bridge had been put in, and then going back on the other side of the river. The engineers were good about quickly putting in those temporary bridges. They could have taken a civilian makeshift ferry across, avoiding the lengthy detour, but the ferry didn't look too good. It was just a wide boat with planks laid crosswise that could accommodate the small European cars, people, and bicycles. On the other side, the only way off the ferry was to go up a temporary ramp on planks laid from the ferry to a stone wall forming part of the river bank. The edge was about six feet above the level of the ferry, so Fred said to his driver, "I'm not in that much of a hurry."

One detour took them through the back country, and he really saw the French farms. Because it was exclusively farm country, their roads all went through farmland and the detour took them on a winding road that really was most interesting. They were on the road about 6:30 or 7:00 in the evening. All the cows were being brought in for milking. Cows there were really good looking but did not look as though they produced much milk. They were being brought in by boys, girls, and men, most of whom wore wooden shoes. None of the fields were fenced, so during the day someone was with the cows at all times. The women took out folding canvas chairs and either knit or crocheted while they watched the cattle.

The farmers' horses were all Percherons. The French never made their load so heavy that the horse had to strain to pull it. The Italians, on the other hand, all seemed to load up their two-wheel carts until the shafts lifted the horse off the ground. When that happened, the Italians would take a little off and then get on and ride forward on the load so that the horse could get more traction. The Italian horses were continually falling down as their loads were just too heavy. But in France they had big, beautiful, sleek horses that were not bothered by excessive loads.

As soon as a town was liberated, out came the flags and bunting. There was no indication where they came from, but hundreds of French and American flags made their appearance. Chains were made of red, white, and blue paper, and of course it was not any trouble to make the French flag which is of three colors. The American flag was everywhere. There were quite a number of homemade American flags. Some would be square rather than oblong. Some would only have about six stars but the thought and sentiment was there.

★ ★ ★

The following excerpt is from *"History of the 64th Fighter Wing"*:
A convoy of trucks bearing Ops 2 moved through

newly-liberated land. The people, farmers and small-town tradesmen, were dazed with their newfound freedom. After the first bewilderment, they became joyous, and as the first American convoys roared through the countryside, the people stood by the roads and shouted their greeting. They stood and cheered. Some of them cried. Tears streamed down their cheeks but their faces were beaming. The tears came from joy, from gratitude. Old and young lined the sides of the road—men and women, girls and boys—and waved frantically at the Americans. They carried flowers and threw them to the soldiers sitting on the heaped high luggage in the trucks. They gave them fruit and eggs, melons and tomatoes, the produce of their farms and gardens.

Soldiers were suspicious when they saw these offerings. In Italy such things had their price. Here they discovered that the people were trying to give these things to them. Such gifts were small expressions of their gratitude. The real expression was in their eyes, in their faces, in the way they waved and shouted, cheered, laughed, yelled and cried. The people brought out champagne, Eau de vie, fine wines they had hoarded for years, and gave them to the soldiers, holding the bottles at arm's length so the men could grab them as the trucks rumbled by.

The spirits of the soldiers rose. They felt good. For the first time since coming overseas they were seeing the reason for Africa, Sicily and Italy. They could observe the effect of freedom on people who had not been free for a long time. The soldiers had seen Italians welcoming them enthusiastically into captured Italian cities, but somehow it had been enthusiasm with reservations. This was different. This was enthusiasm without restraint.

Biol

An experience presented itself that Fred never expected in Biol and because he had a large glass of beer, he had his eye open for a urinal. They had them everywhere and anywhere because, if they were not, the nearest wall would be used. The urinals were a metal, round wall with legs that held it up about 15 inches from the ground. Feet could be seen of the people using the structure. They were for men only. He located one by seeing the sign *Hommes*, which meant *men*. This one was in a traffic island in the middle of the street and below the street level. He went down, and just as he got inside the door there was an old lady sitting there knitting. She apparently kept the place clean and collected two francs from each person who entered.

★ ★ ★

He had a letter from Esta in which she mentioned that Italian prisoners were wearing American uniforms. He could understand why it had been done. There was a large stock of uniforms and it would be too much to design and manufacture separate clothing. But even so, it angered every American soldier. They had been taught to be proud of the American uniform and to believe that only an American could wear it. The French Army had been fully equipped and clothed in American equipment and clothing for quite some time. Their insignia was the only difference. In Corsica the French people actually criticized the Americans for wearing the French uniform and made statements to the effect that the Americans ought to be ashamed of themselves for wearing the French uniforms when France was so poor and America was so rich. Imagine that!

Don't think that Fred was being critical of the policy. Just imagine the detail and organization that would have to be done if there had to be special uniforms. A German General once said that, if he were to choose his enemy, he would always choose Allies. Separate supplies and supply dumps for every nation causes far more grief than just one.

There was another way of looking at allowing another nation to use our supplies. When we first saw the French using our equipment, and very often not using it right, our boys were burned up. The way to look at it though was that if the French were not in our uniforms and using our equipment, our own boys would be. And, if there happened to be casualties, who would be best in the uniform, French or American? The answer was brought home much closer when Fred saw French dead in American uniforms.

★ ★ ★

A General told how he and another General were parked in a town, sitting in a jeep. At the time, a convoy of troops was passing through and the people were throwing flowers, fruit, etc. to the boys in the trucks. An old lady was trying to toss tomatoes into the trucks on the opposite side of the street from the jeep. Her timing was not very good and she missed every truck. But the tomatoes did come over to the other side, and they did come in and around the jeep with the two Generals.

★ ★ ★

Convery was visiting with an AA officer, a first lieutenant, who complimented the Air Force on the Early Warning that was received at Casino, telling how it helped him and his boys on the guns. Another time, when Convery was having a glass of wine in a cafe one evening, several AA officers there, who were at Casino, said the same thing.

★ ★ ★

Fred was really proud of what took place in March of '44. The Early Warning Section had been able to give the warning of the incoming Jerry planes to guns 75 miles from the Ops Room, which made it possible for them to do some good shooting, and that shooting changed Jerry's mind about sending in his planes on a number of occasions.

★ ★ ★

There were times when Fred didn't feel good. His stomach felt as rotten as though he had eaten a can of pork and beans without removing the tin wrapper. About the best way to describe it was that his stomach just felt tired. They had been eating canned food for so long that a diet of fresh food would seem like heaven. They did have some fresh food, but even so, it seemed that the cooks made it taste like canned food.

★ ★ ★

The little village that they occupied was really pretty when the sun was out. There were only five or six buildings and no streets at all. They made a road by driving over the grass several times. Try and imagine some very old town with its wide streets, maybe New Orleans. Take about six of the larger homes in a row, put grass in for the streets and sidewalks, add some trees, place about a dozen geese on the grass, arrange the whole thing up on a hill, and you'd have that place. Oh yes, at the end of the row of buildings, set a large church with a high steeple, the entire structure being of stone. The church was very old, having been founded in the ninth century.

People from all over walked to the church which had quite a congregation. They must have come from miles around in order to support a church of that size.

In the steeple there was a clock. The bells rang every quarter hour. One would think that they would put in chimes to ring the time, but that was not done. There were four tones (Do, Re, Mi, So). "Re, Mi, So" was rung for the quarter hour, repeated once for the half-hour, three times for the quarter-hour, and four times for the hour. Then the hour was rung by the "Do" bell. It really got rather monotonous. However, it was noticed that the sequence had been changed to "Mi, So, Re" for the quarter-hours.

* * *

Convery's papers for promotion went in all right, but something had to be added which should have been included when they were first sent in. It seemed to take forever for those things to clear the channels. If it worked, okay, and if it didn't it was still okay.

* * *

In September the nights were chilly, and to provide some heat in the office they used the burner of a gasoline kitchen stove. It worked fine, but to have something that would radiate heat, a big cast iron kettle was put over the burner, upside down. It really got hot and acted just like an airtight heater. The cast iron pot was about 15 inches wide and 12 inches high.

* * *

Captain Butler was quite an individual. He had spent about seven years studying French, so he spoke French very well and got along just fine with all of the French people. He came from near Boston and was a stereo-typical Bostonian, inclined to be a bit prissy but not in the way you might think. He was very careful about his clothes and kept himself dressed at his best all the time. He smoked and enjoyed a drink but was inclined to be fussy and sort of feminine. He had been the Adjutant for a long time. Consequently, he had the idea that he knew everything and was very positive in his statements. However, at any time there was a question about some point, all one had to do was to offer to make a bet, involving money, and he would back right down. He was a good Joe and everybody liked him, but sometimes he did things in a funny way.

* * *

Lieutenant Temple, who has been mentioned before, was the wire officer and came from around Chicago. He was a little shorter than Fred. He was quite an individual and liked by everyone. Ninety percent of the time he would have a cheek full of chewing tobacco and very often a cigar at the same time. He and

Fred worked very close together. He usually drove his own jeep and was a very reckless driver.

When planning to lay his wire communications, Temple had to find out just where the railroad lines and the commercial lines were. He always made as much use as possible of the lines that were already in. He had a habit of trying to drive a jeep in heavy traffic at about 45 miles an hour and, at the same time, keep looking over the pole lines and watching for signs of some railroad for his telegraph lines. Can you imagine taking a ride with him? If he had a passenger in the back seat, he would turn clear around to talk to him. However, he helped Fred out quite a bit to get communications going while in Italy. He would give the location of a point or place where a connection could be made for a line to the Ops Room. It then was Fred's job to get that information to AA Brigade Headquarters, who in turn would arrange for all of their AA guns to hook into the network.

After one trip, Convery got back a little before supper and was sure glad to get back. It had been raining nearly all the time he had been gone. Riding in a jeep in the rain was not fun. It would not have been so bad if it were not for the side angles that went along with it. A unit would set up its camp near a highway, and even though the area would be grassy, the whole area soon became a sea of mud. The trucks would chew right through the sod and really make it a mess. Or, when the trucks would leave, they carried the mud along on their tires and running gear, and it gradually dropped off onto the pavement for miles and miles. It would be quite thick near the camps and then gradually lessen. Consequently, if they were in a convoy or following a truck, and Lord knows there were a lot of them, they would be covered by a fine mist of mud and water that settled on them like snow. That is what he had to contend with all day. In addition to that, the swipes on the jeeps worked by hand, which was a nuisance and were old and dry and did not work very well.

★ ★ ★

On another trip they followed along a very pretty little river that looked like it never changed its level because there were no sandbars or washed out places anywhere. It was just like a long narrow lake of moving water. It appeared that way because the river was used before the war for small canal boats. The river had small dams about every half-mile to mile that backed the water up to make it navigable. Then, at each dam there was a small lock that let the canal boats pass the dam. Sometimes the canal would be beside the river with a lock at each end of the canal so that the boats could use the river. It was really very picturesque with the grass growing on the banks right down to the water.

Whenever Fred went anywhere, he took along everything he might need to stay as long as necessary—his folding cot, sleeping bag, blankets, a box of rations, a Coleman single- burner stove for making coffee, and toilet articles. That way he could stay anywhere at any time and did not have to get to his destination by meal time. One rainy day they pulled into a gravel pit out of the wind and fixed themselves a very good lunch.

Once they stopped at the 439th and had lunch with the old outfit. They told him about the boy whose tommy gun went off while he was sleeping in his pup tent, at his first assignment in Africa. He went into the hospital, and then when he got out, he came back to the outfit rather than going into a replacement depot. He said that he particularly wanted to come back to the outfit because he liked Convery, who was quite flattered.

The "rule of three" seems to have applied to the boy. While in Italy, a jeep he was riding in went off a bridge. He was not hurt but one of the other occupants was killed. Then later on, while the outfit was doing infantry duty on the front line in Italy, he, Thompson, was shot between the eyes. Fred certainly felt badly about it because Thompson was a mighty fine boy. Lieutenant Kersey was right behind him at the time, and the bullet hit Kersey after it killed Thompson. The "rule of three" had many applications. It was very bad to ever light three on a match.

Fred was sleeping in a tent even though it was darn cold sometimes and always wet! His tent had been in position for ten days and in the same place. The ground should have been a little dry under it but it wasn't. He had to keep his shoes off the ground; otherwise they got wet clear through, absorbing the moisture from the ground. He was not sorry he was sleeping in a tent though, because in one of the buildings being used for offices there was a large room on the third floor that about 25 or 30 officers were using for their quarters. At first not very many were in there, but others gradually moved in and it became quite crowded. The room was the full length and width of the building. Being large, the one stove did not heat sufficiently and the room was always cold. The people sleeping next to the windows didn't want their windows open and those who were not near the windows wanted them open during sleeping hours. A couple of officers caught colds and then they all had colds. Fred's tent was damp, but he was snug and warm with his Perfection oil stove. It heated up rapidly and he could always dress and undress in a warm place, which was really something in that kind of weather.

★ ★ ★

The following is taken from *"History of the 64th Fighter Wing"*:

> While Boxcar (the code name for Wing Headquarters) was at Dole, it assisted in one of the most dramatic interceptions ever made by the Wing. Beginning about 21 September 1944, both control centers daily reported an unknown track, from the direction of Stuttgart and to the Spanish border, between 2100 and 2200 hours. A similar track appeared each morning between 0330 and 0430, going in the opposite direction. General Barcus believed these flights to be hostile. However, they could be something other than hostile because the plane was not flying fast enough to be a military craft and it had no fighter protection of any

kind. Higher Headquarters were contacted and there was no information of any kind about its identity.

General Barcus directed that Major Goldsein and other controllers plan to use the 415th Night Fighter Squadron and make an interception control which would not require radio transmission by the intercepting Beaufighter (a Beaufighter is a night fighter plane). It would get all the information needed for making contact with the unknown or hostile flight. Radio silence by the aircraft was necessary so that it would escape detection by the enemy plane and by the usually efficient German "Y" service.

The mission, originally scheduled for 26 September, was prevented by bad weather, and the flight was laid on for the next night. At 2000 hours on the 27th, a Beaufighter piloted by Capt. Augspurger was airborne. Jerry was not long in appearing. The Delaware radar station picked him up at 2007 and within two minutes the track was identified as hostile. At 2010 the interception began, and at 2031 the pilot announced the successful contact, "Eureka! It's a Jerry!" The FW-200 transport went down in a huge ball of fire, hit the ground and exploded violently. Officers of the Wing, including General Barcus drove immediately to the scene of the crash and recovered from the wreckage documents and material of great value.

The interception was particularly valuable and a significant Allied victory, because it frustrated the enemy's attempt to use in Spain one of its last remaining sources of intelligence of the outside world. After 27 September the Germans rarely attempted to send transports on the Spanish run and then only during the poorest flying weather. The above interception was planned in such a way that the plane would be brought down as close as possible to Dole, so that General Barcus could make a personal inspection of the downed plane.

★ ★ ★

Fred received another package from Esta and in it was some popping corn and a Hershey bar. He popped some of the popcorn over his Coleman stove about 4:30 and took it over to the Officers' Club, where the boys had it with their drinks before supper. It sure went over big. He used a coffee pot to pop it. The coffee pot made a real good corn popper.

★ ★ ★

In October most of the days were wet and cold. It was darn miserable riding in a jeep. For a number of days Fred was really under the weather with a bad cold. He was in an area where it was ordered that everyone had to wear a helmet at all times. He had gone to a barbershop to get a haircut about 4:00 in the afternoon. Besides the haircut, he had a shampoo. It so happened that when he left the shop he drove directly to the unit where he was staying—only 9 kilometers away. It was quite cold, and he did not have his wool cap that was worn under the helmets in cold weather. The helmet made a regular air scoop and the air whistled around his head. The next morning he had a beautiful cold.

★ ★ ★

His promotion was traveling around. The reason it did not come through with some others was because being an AA officer it had to go to AA Headquarters. Also, being in France, they were in what was called the European Theatre of Operations. When the papers were sent in, they were in Italy and the Mediterranean Theatre of Operations. Apparently the papers had been sent back to be started again.

★ ★ ★

Convery had to make a trip into Lyons. A second lieutenant heard that he was going on the trip and asked whether he could hitch a ride. Apparently he had just one thing in mind because every so often he would repeat a French phrase someone had given him, "*Ville vou cushay Avec mwa.*" The spelling could be wrong. It meant "*Will you sleep with me.*"

★ ★ ★

Fred was at his desk when an officer from one of the Operations Rooms called and said to hold the line for a minute. He was surprised to hear none other than Harry Overly, Esta's brother. They had quite a visit, even though they were about 140 miles apart. He was not far away from the Operations Room that had been set up at Lourdes. He had seen a direction sign for the 64th Fighter Wing Headquarters and managed to get to the Operations Room by inquiry at several Headquarters. He said he was well but uncomfortably cold. Fred told him that should not bother him too much because he was a supply officer. He said that was all over and that he was doing regular duty with a mortar platoon. He already had credit for a couple 88s.

Harry always used field telephones which were used by the infantry to string wires (communication) within their own units. The individual telephones contained batteries, and the range of the field telephone was, at best, about 14 miles. Communication systems within the Air Force Operations Rooms back and forth were in some cases radio telephones, which were becoming very good and very clear. That was what they talked over. Harry could not believe that Fred was 140 miles away.

★ ★ ★

Being the Ack-Ack Officer caused friendly cracks every once in awhile because there had been a number of cases of wrong identification of aircraft and our own Ack-Ack had shot down our own planes. It was never on purpose, of course. Then our own planes would retaliate and bomb and strafe our own troops by mistake. It did not happen frequently, but when it did, it caused plenty of comment. It was not happening as much then as it had eighteen months before.

One time a number of troops were cut off and supplies had to be flown in to them. The weather was really bad, but the pilots did a wonderful job. One pilot, after dropping the supplies, was flying out on instruments and hit a tree. Not enough damage was done to bring him down, but even so he was just able to get back to his base. He said that he was all through flying after that, but after he had a couple of drinks, he flew again the next day. The next day was bad too, and while flying low over an area, he was shot at by mistake and the plane was brought down. That time he had to bail out. Fred took a lot of razzing that day. But the very next day a pilot made a mistake in recognition and shot down one of our planes. That sort of evened up the score. Those things happened and were really too bad, but they were just things that happened during a war.

November 1 was "payday" and Fred drew the regular monthly amount of $520.10 less $320.00 for Esta, $8.10 and $22.50 for miscellaneous deductions, for a net of $69.50 to him for pocket money. He drew one grade higher in pay all the time he was in the Service because he had considerable longevity. In November 1944, he was drawing the pay of a major, although he was a captain at the time.

Lourdes, Near Nancy

Headquarters moved to Lourdes, a small village near Nancy. A large two-story building was taken over for the Ops Room, offices and dining room. Fred was all set and living with a French family in the same manner as the winter of 1943 when he was billeted in Italy. The family was not as well-to-do as the Funnaris, but he believed that he was going to enjoy them just as much. He had a room that he shared with a major by the name of Cooper who had just been sent to the Wing as an Army liaison officer for ground situation work. Lourdes was a typical small French town. The homes were clean, but the streets were cobblestones and mud. Some of the homes had barns as part of the house.

Often, Major Cooper and Fred went down to their room about 9:00 p.m. from the Headquarters building and spent the rest of the evening visiting with the Colignones, their landlord and his wife. Neither Cooper nor Fred could speak French. Most of the conversation was with gestures and one word at a time. With the aid of a French dictionary that Esta sent Fred while he was in Africa, it was surprising how much information could be passed. It really was a lot of fun. Monsieur Colignone worked in a large store nearby and had been there since the last war. His wife was quite buxom and real nice.

One morning Fred noticed a funny sound before he got up and couldn't figure out what it was. It sounded like a rat chewing on a timber, and maybe that is what it was. Anyway, he noticed on his way to breakfast that the room next door was a cow barn in the same building. He had not noticed it before because the doors had been closed, and it looked like the rest of the house.

The Colignones had a two-story house and used both floors. They slept upstairs and had a room downstairs that was a combination kitchen and dining room. Cooper and Fred's room, which was right next to the kitchen, was probably the dining room at one time but had been made into a bedroom. Those were the only two rooms downstairs. However, in back was one room that was used for the storage of potatoes, fruit, squash, etc. The room was not floored and was also the wine cellar. There were four or five barrels of wine stored back there. Next to that room was another room that was not floored. That room had rabbits on one side and chickens on the other. Everything was entirely inside the house. However, there was no running water in the house. All of the water had to be carried from the town square a short distance away. With no running water, there was no inside plumbing. However, there was an inside toilet though, believe it or not. It was outdoor plumbing moved inside. What happened and where it went was a mystery to Fred. All around it and outside of the toilet room, which was small, the floor was of concrete. In back of the building was a dirt bank forming the back wall in which Colignone stored, or rather aged, his bottled wine and liquor. It was quite a building with all of that on the first floor. Strange as it may seem, Fred's room was very nice and clean, with electric lights, and a metal and tile stove.

The stove was not very large, approximately three feet high and one foot by two feet. It was covered completely with tile on the four sides and top. The fire box was very small, just a little bit larger than a normal shoe box. A small amount of wood in the fire box really kept the room warm. Once the stove became hot, the tile stayed warm throwing off heat for a long time.

★ ★ ★

On another trip, Fred and his driver got caught in a rain storm and got soaking wet. So, rather than sleeping out, they located a hotel in a small village in the mountains. The hotel was not much, but even so, it was comfortable. They asked whether they could get supper there, and understood the hotel keeper to say that he had no food (he spoke a little English). So, they fixed their own meal in their room. About the time they were through, they were sent word that dinner would be served in ten minutes. Well, there was nothing to do but go down and eat. It turned out that the place was sort of a boarding house because, in the dining room which they had not seen before, were quite a number of people, about 25. Fred could not tell who they were or where they were from and could only conjecture.

Previously he had heard that, in this section of the country, there were a great number of refugees from Germany and believed that in the group there were at least a few. There was a French officer and a young boy about fifteen. The officer was dressed in the French Army uniform, so he knew that he had just recently taken it out of storage, probably a few days before. It likely had been in storage since the French surrendered. He could not have been part of the French Army that had been going along with us because all of the officers and men of that Army were in American clothing.

There was a couple that were very well dressed. The woman was black haired and plainly dressed in dark clothing, as though she did not want to be noticed. The man was slightly bald and inclined to be heavy set. He wore glasses and had a closely-cut dark mustache. Neither of them seemed to talk much. He seemed to be more interested in what he was eating than in anything else. He ate while continually watching all that was in front of him. He seemed to decide what the next mouthful was going to be in order to have it ready when he had swallowed what he was already chewing. Actually, Fred didn't recall seeing the woman eat but was sure she must have.

Sitting at the next table were two Frenchmen, both of whom had large, long, white mustaches. They both wore berets while they were eating, which was a Jewish custom. At the next table was a gray-haired old lady. Her hair was her outstanding feature.

It was done up in hundreds of tiny ringlets, in such a quantity that at first he had the impression that her hair was bushy, but the more he looked, it took shape. Her hair was so white that it was not white, gray, or silver color, but had a color all its own. There was another gray-haired lady who was eating alone. Her hair was pulled back close to her head and was tied in a tight knot in back. When the waitress had trouble understanding them, she came over and asked in English whether she could help. It was surprising to hear her speak English.

The weather became stormy and bad. Fred was glad that he had a dry and comfortable room to live in. His bed was a good one. In addition to covers, there was a feather comforter. It was not large. He had seen them around in various rooms. They all were about the same in size—just about the width of the bed and made square.

★ ★ ★

Major Cooper was also a Coast Artillery officer. Fred asked him whether he knew anyone by the name of Edwin W. Jones. He knew Jones very well. In fact, they were in the same regiment and lived in the same town. Before Fred told him all about Jones, he asked whether Jones was still drinking as much as ever. Cooper said that even though they were in the same regiment and lived in the same town they did not associate socially at all, because he considered himself in an entirely different class. He said that Jones had always done a lot of drinking, and he was not surprised at what Fred had to tell him.

★ ★ ★

An afternoon proved to be real exciting. The weather broke just after lunch, and it turned out to be real nice, with clear skies, no rain, and no fog. Consequently, the General sent a number of squadrons of planes on various missions. While they were up, the weather changed, rapidly closing in. Getting a bunch of planes back to their various bases in a case like that was really difficult, because the controllers had to keep track of where the planes were and where they had to go. They had to get the information to the pilots in order to help them back to their bases.

★ ★ ★

Fred celebrated his 41st birthday in a big way. He didn't go anywhere, didn't make any plans, but after he left with Major Cooper to go to Headquarters, he began to think that he ought to do something. He didn't know just what. On their way back to their billet, Fred told him that the day was his birthday. He told the Colignones, and, of course, they offered their congratulations. Madame Colignone gave him a French type kiss—that is on the cheek—and she turned for him to give her a kiss on the cheek. That was the custom. Then Marcelle, the twelve-year-old daughter gave him one and turned her cheek. With all offering their congratulations, he decided to have a party. He got out his one bottle of champagne from the assortment he had purchased about a week before, and Madame Colignone got out some glasses. They all sat down at the kitchen table and had a party. She got out a couple boxes of crackers that looked like Nabisco's. She had been saving them for a long time for some special occasion. She also opened a jar of peaches that she had canned. Both were treasured items because Nabisco's could not be purchased and the peaches were canned with sugar which was no longer available. Fred had three candles stored away for future use and got those out. They had a birthday party after all. He couldn't help but think of the birthday party he had the previous year at Bizerte, just before they left for Italy, when he was wondering where he was going to spend his next birthday.

★ ★ ★

General Kelly, AA General of the 7th Army, came to see General Barcus. Among other things, he came to check up on the Captain's promotion. He took copies of the papers to find out what was taking so long. Fred talked with him for awhile. He seemed very pleased with the way everything was going. He made one or two suggestions, and when asked about the suggestions, he said that he didn't want to change anything that had been done or any of the procedures—that everything was up to Fred to handle any way he wanted. Later, General Barcus was going through Fred's office and said, "General Kelly certainly said a lot of nice things about you the other day."

The Wing was running four different Control Centers, and there was AA personnel at each one. They were handling the Early Warning to the AA guns for not only the 7th Army but also for the 1st French Army and some of the 3rd Army. Also, a lot that were not a part of any of them. The Control Rooms were scattered all over France.

★ ★ ★

One afternoon Cooper and Fred were invited to the Colignones after lunch for dessert. They were not quite sure just what was to take place, but they went. After dinner at noon, they went down to the house where the Colignones were waiting. They took them upstairs to their dining room, which was furnished very nicely, and sat them down at the table.

She first brought out an almond pie. Fred and Cooper saw her getting it ready the night before. She had been saving the almonds since before the war, about four years. Almonds were not raised in France. Monsieur Colignone shelled the almonds for her. She then blanched them and put them into a bowl of cream she obtained from a neighbor. That was mixed with some sugar she had been saving, purchased on the black market. The whole bowl was put away to stand overnight. In the morning she baked the pie, which was open-faced with a thin filling. The filling she had made the night before was mixed with an egg in the morning. It was like a custard pie but not so thick.

Then, Monsieur Colignone brought out some Vin Rouge (red wine). The bottle was all dusty and old looking, and the cork was sealed with beeswax. The bottle really looked like it had been put away for a long time. He said he had hidden it in a cave to keep it from being taken by the Germans. It was really good. They had two glasses of the wine.

Then, Madame Colignone brought out a cake which was baked in a ring and was about three inches high and three inches thick. When she made a cake or baked a pie crust, she had to take the brown flour that she could get and sift out the white, leaving the bran, which was used for breakfast food or fed to the chickens. Her stove was just about worn out. To finish her baking she had to take some coals out of the firebox and put them on the floor of the oven. The cake was soaked with brandy. It was sort of a plain cake, but with the brandy it was different from anything ever tasted before. The brandy was not strong but it was potent. The cake was almost soupy and just about fell apart. It had to be eaten with a spoon. To go with the brandy-soaked cake, Monsieur Colignone brought out a bottle of champagne he had also been saving in his cave since the war began. Fred had never tasted better champagne. It was really delightful, a light golden color with just the right amount of twang.

A couple of hours later, after a lot of conversation, Madame Colignone made some coffee from the coffee Esta had sent. Coffee was quite a delicacy for the Colignones. It was another item that they had not been able to get for four years. They added Eau de vie, which means water of life. The GIs called it liquid lightning. It was a form of brandy but about ten times stronger. It was a French specialty that most Frenchmen drank all the time. Made from small prunes, it was allowed to ferment and then was distilled. It was all right if you wanted something to set you on fire, but as far as Fred was concerned, he would rather have drunk equal parts of gasoline and turpentine.

Following the coffee with the Eau de Vie, they had to drink some straight Eau de Vie. Then there was more talk and they listened to the radio for news. By that time, it was close to 5:00, and it was time for them to go to the mess to eat. So, Monsieur Colignone brought out a bottle of vermouth and gave them a couple of glasses, just so they would have a good appetite for dinner. Each wine was served in a different type of glass. She really had beautiful glassware.

Needless to say, by that time Fred was beginning to get a beautiful glow, and it was just as well that supper was in the offing because he could not have taken much more.

* * *

There was a village distillery located in Lourdes. In France, no liquor was taxed unless it was sold in a bottle. To avoid any tax, or as much tax as possible, villagers would distill their own brandies by fermenting their fruits. They then took the mash to the village distillery. The distiller distilled the fermented juices, returned the distilled liquor to the individual, keeping half for himself. Colignone took Fred to the small still where he took his mash. It looked like a moonshiner's. He then took him to the dirt-covered bank behind his house where he stored his bottled liquor. The Eau de Vie that he served had been left there for seven years. He never used all of the seven-year stock, always leaving a few bottles for future use.

* * *

One day Fred left Lourdes about 10:00 and was taking care of some details in Nancy. About 11:30 he got a call from Headquarters. The duty officer (AA) told him that his brother-in-law was there and in the office. He told the duty officer to have him sit right there and wait for him to get back and they would have lunch together. He came back by 12:10 and found Harry waiting. They had a really good visit, but it was too short. After a lunch of meat loaf, mashed potatoes, gravy and corn, which Harry enjoyed, they went down to Fred's room for coffee. Harry really enjoyed the hot coffee because he said they had not had very much.

Fred decided to take the afternoon off and really visit with him, but Fred had two calls to Colonel Jackson's office and had to go to Headquarters twice during the time Harry was there. Harry had to be back by 4:00, so that meant he had to leave at 3:30. He had hitch-hiked his way over from near Lunneville where his

44th Infantry Regiment was located. Fred sent him back with the jeep in order for him to stay longer and not have to hitch his way back. Harry had been in the hospital for five days with hemorrhoids and was due to be discharged. He got leave from the hospital to look Fred up because he thought that Fred would have a tough time finding him, which was undoubtedly true.

Another reason he wanted to look Fred up and why he had to get back to his outfit that night was because he understood his outfit was going to push off the next day. Fred opened his bottle of whiskey, and they had several drinks in between Fred's trips to Headquarters.

Harry said that the worst part about the war was the long nights in a foxhole. They had to get into their foxholes and dugouts at night and stay there until daylight. It got dark around 6:00 and that made a long night out of it. They didn't dare get out of their dugouts and walk around, because if they did they were liable to find a hand grenade in their pocket. They even used their helmets for pots. He had his dugout blacked out and did not have any light. Fred gave him five candles since he almost always had light of some sort and didn't need them. He also gave him an electric lantern. Harry was very happy with that. Fred gave him some *Chronicles*. They were all dated before Harry even left the States, which was Labor Day, but one of them was a Saturday issue, and Harry took it for the funnies. He said that the men went crazy about the funnies. Harry took along a Sunday *PI* (*Seattle Post Intelligencer*) that had arrived the day before.

Fred was looking for the candles in his box of stuff and came across one of those extra wristwatch bands Esta had sent, and gave it to him. He was pleased with that and put his watch on it right away. Harry also told Fred how cold it was and the job that it was to keep warm. Fred then gave him a knitted hood. It was a wool OD knit hood that had a muffler knit onto the back side. It really was a honey because it not only kept the head warm under the hood of an overcoat, but it had the muffler along with it. Fred only used it once when he was making a trip in the jeep and thought that Harry could get a lot more use out of it than he could. Harry thought it was just the thing. Later, he told Fred that sometimes at night he loaned his overcoat with the hood to one of his men while on guard because the hood worked so well. Fred also gave him one of his bottles of Cognac. They had not been able to get much of anything of that kind up there and he thought he could put it to good use. Harry kept track of the birthdays of his men. Three of the men shared the same birthday, so he got them all together and gave them a drink from the bottle that he had. Harry was becoming a darn good officer!

★ ★ ★

In Lourdes, the same as all of the other villages around, clothes were washed at one central place in the village. The troughs, like horse troughs, were made from concrete and covered with a roof. The water ran through them continuously. On the edge of the troughs were concrete washboards. All the women took their clothes there to wash. It was quite a job and it looked like they would freeze their hands off. They brought their clothes to the wash-trough with steam coming from the boiled clothes. That kept their hands warm for a little while anyway.

Village laundry in Lourdes, France

Madame Colignone would not take any money from Fred for doing his washing and ironing, as well as cleaning his room every day. She even pressed wool shirts and trousers after they were cleaned. Fred showed her how to put in a military press, and she did it perfectly. She had an electric iron, but usually the power was not strong enough to heat the iron so she used sadirons heated on the stove.

Once, Marcelle had an infected thumb and Fred planned to take her to the medical officer if it got any worse. They appreciated things like that and the things that were given to them, but that seemed so little in exchange. Besides that, Madam Colignone built a fire in the stove every night just before the men came home. Of course, the room was paid for by the government, but the cleaning and washing were to be paid by officer tenants.

The Colignones invited Major Cooper and Fred to an evening tea party. They were asked into the kitchen, and she brought out the tea Fred had given her. She made the tea in the regular way, but in addition to sugar she put in a teaspoon of rum. It was different than anything he had ever tasted. It was not enough to make the tea taste too strong but just enough to give it a wonderful flavor. Then another pot of tea was made, and besides the sugar a spoonful of honey was added and a spoonful of rum. It was quite sweet. Madame Colignone added a spoonful of thick cream to Marcelle's tea.

Major Cooper had not been over there long enough to appreciate anything like the Fig Newtons and popcorn that Esta had sent. Anyone who had been overseas very long really appreciated Fig Newtons and all other goodies sent from home. As far as the Major was concerned, those were just regular things and nothing to get excited about. It sort of burned Fred up a bit but he was certain Cooper would learn in time. Cooper was beginning to mope a bit, just like the rest all did. Fred knew that it would not be long before he would be like the rest with an "overseas pallor."

That is sort of a frame of mind that one got into which carried on and on and on. You just put up with everything and did not think too much about being away from home. It was an anesthetic that carried through to the end and prevented homesickness, wife sickness, and all other forms of longing. It was the only thing to do and still get along with everyone else.

* * *

Again Fred saw the barge canals that were quite interesting, although they were out of action. They ran across France and at one time handled quite a bit of traffic-hauling coal, ore, etc. to the steel mills. The canals were out of action because so many of the locks had been damaged. The water was gone and the barges were resting on the bottom. They appeared to be motor operated and not drawn by horses. They were long, narrow and quite flat— also quite low in order to go under the bridges. In several places the canal could be seen running beside the river but quite a bit higher. Sometimes it would turn and cross right over the river on a bridge. At one place the canal wound around and crossed itself.

* * *

That promotion of Fred's was getting almost embarrassing. It had been so long since the papers first went in that it was grape-vine news. Almost every day someone would ask when it was coming. His only answer was that he didn't know and that he would only believe it when he saw it.

* * *

Major Cooper got up one morning and said, "I didn't sleep very well last night. You know, I dreamed of every girl I have ever known. I don't know why I did that—I have never done it be-fore." Being overseas was beginning to have its effect.

* * *

November 1944 . . . It finally came through . . . at supper the General called Fred to his table and told him his promotion to Major had come.

However, Fred did not feel any different but was happy. It

was in the late summer of 1942 when the first situation developed that interrupted Fred's promotion to major. Then came the Jones affair and Fred's release as Executive Officer of the 439th AA Battalion in December of 1943 because Major Jones was sent back to the Battalion. In June of 1944 papers were again sent in but came back because the Air Force could not promote an Army officer. Next, after being sent through the right channels, the papers again came back because the Wing was part of the invasion of Southern France and had moved from the Mediterranean Theater of Operations to the European Theatre. Again the papers were sent in and that time they finally went all the way through. All the time from December of 1943 Convery was in the position assignment of lieutenant colonel.

★ ★ ★

A few days later a message was left for Fred from a Red Cross man at the 51st Evacuation Hospital. He had called to say that Lt. Harry Overly was there. At first he thought Harry was back at the hospital where he had been the week before with the hemorrhoids. But when he started to call, he could tell by the exchanges that he was not there. It then occurred to him that Harry would not be in that particular hospital unless he had been wounded because they would not have sent him that far for a short treatment of hemorrhoids. He finally got through to the Red Cross and was told that Harry had been wounded in his foot. He asked whether Harry would be going back to his outfit, and was told that he probably would be going to a convalescent hospital and that he would not be there very long because an evacuation hospital kept the patients moving on as fast as possible.

Fred went to see Harry at the hospital. Arriving there about 11:30, they had lunch together, and he left about 1:30. It was a good thing he went when he did because Harry was to be evacuated to a rear area hospital at 2:00 and he might have missed him entirely.

Harry had quite an experience and certainly was lucky—he

knew it, too. He and several other men had dived into a slit trench during some shelling. A shell landed in a slit trench just a few feet away and killed two men. Two other men nearby got pieces of shell fragments in their legs and were wounded worse than Harry. He just happened to have his foot sticking up a bit and got a small piece in the back of the middle toe of his right foot.

When Harry left on the day he came to see Fred, things started to happen as soon as he got back to his outfit. He did not get any sleep until he got to the hospital, and when they gave him some shots, he slept for eighteen hours. His foot bothered him quite a bit. He needed surgery and did not get any treatment for a number of hours. His foot had begun to swell, and he was given penicillin shots which immediately took the swelling down. He expected to be in the hospital for a couple of months. His foot did not bother him unless he had it down, that is, by sitting or standing with crutches. They went to the mess hall together. Fred remarked about how well he got along on his crutches. He said that this was the fourth time he had something happen to his foot. It was not as easy for him to go with Fred as he said, but he insisted on going. They ate as fast as they could in order for him to get back to his cot as soon as possible. Harry said that during those three or four days he had only eaten about once a day and missed one or two of those. He just could not get filled up when he got into the hospital. For one thing, he didn't feel like eating when he arrived, and then he was asleep for so long. No wonder he was hungry.

Harry told of an incident that made Fred feel pretty good. Harry had put the candles in his overcoat pocket and had forgotten about them. The second night of the attack, they were shelled pretty bad. The battalion aid station was set up in a French barn, and the place was filled with wounded men lying on the floor. In fact, there were so many that a number were lying outside. He was there and found that it was difficult for the aid station personnel to work because they did not have any light.

Something had happened to the power equipment. They were having a tough time taking care of the wounded. Harry happened to remember the candles in his pocket and gave them to the aid men. The candles were lit and they were able to work all night long by the light of those candles. Harry said that the candles must have saved any number of lives.

They had a captured German doctor working on the wounded. He worked right along with the rest, on both the American and German soldiers. The doctor still thought that Germany would win.

While visiting with Harry, the Red Cross girl came around to see whether there was anything she could do. She passed on some local gossip that was causing quite a bit of excitement in the hospital. That morning a brand new baby had been found in the latrine. No one knew where it came from or how it got there. The nurses were all excited over it. Working on nothing but men all that time, a baby was quite a change for the nurses. It was a girl!

★ ★ ★

Lieutenant Mets, Fred's new roommate, and he were talking to the Colignones about the Christmas customs there. Instead of hanging up stockings, the youngsters all put their shoes around the stove or fireplace. He had always thought that the custom of hanging up stockings was a custom carried over from Europe.

★ ★ ★

Gene Wertz and Fred went into active duty at the same time with the old 205th. He was in Fred's outfit, and while they were in California he recommended that Gene be sent to Officers' Training School. Later on, Gene came to the 457th with Fred, and then sometime after that he left the 457th in England for the 554th AA Automatic Weapons Battalion. The following was taken from a letter from Gene to Fred:

"We have been bucking the center of the line ever since we came over and have all sorts of missions, mostly with the Field Artillery but at times with the

Infantry and then with the Combat Engineers, all making for lots of moves and working closely in operations. So far we have not done too badly in all things concerned. At times in Normandy, when we were hedge hopping along, I wasn't so sure. I just can't seem to feel at home with those darn shells whistling over and plopping around. As for snipers, the only live ones I have seen taken were seven out of a church steeple, and I don't know if they lasted longer than a short march down the road. The outfit that took them had just had their aid station personnel all killed by a German patrol."

★ ★ ★

Newspaper clipping from *Stars & Stripes Weekly*:
"NAZIS KEPT COMING CLOSER
BUT A LONE YANK WAITED . . ."

With the Eighth Inf. Div.—The Germans were counter-attacking and were throwing everything they had at the dazed and almost helpless American platoon. There was nothing the Yanks could do but stick to their slit trenches and wait.

The Jerries were only 200 yards away. Then men saw a lone American figure creeping out of his trench, carrying a Browning automatic rifle. The men watched him crawl forward, saw him reach a point of vantage. He flattened himself into the ground and took aim. Then he waited. The men of his platoon could no more than hope. The burp guns came closer and closer and lead was kicking up the dirt all around, but the lone soldier didn't budge. He felt at his side and found the six full BAR clips he had brought along.

★ ★ ★

NAZIS FELL LIKE DUCKPINS

The Jerries came into view, bobbing up from everywhere. The man tightened his finger on the trigger and the BAR started spurting lead. The Jerries fell like duckpins. They began to retreat.

As a result of his action the company was able to rally and assume a better position, which finally led to the capture of Hill 88 and the fortress of Brest, which the hill overlooked.

The man who stood off the determined German threat was 27-year-old Pfc. Howard Faulder, of Springfield, Ohio. Recently he was awarded the Silver Star by Major Gen. Donald A. Stroh, Eighth Div. Commander.

★ ★ ★

The village of Lourdes must have been there for several hundred years and was probably the same then as it was 200 years ago. There was nothing pretty about the buildings that were all square and built next to each other like paving blocks.

The streets were not paved and there were only a few sidewalks. Each house had its barn. At the edges of the streets were cobblestone gutters for the rain and other waters. Usually there was a small brown stream in the gutters that came from either the barns or the manure piles that were outside each barn. There were only two places for the women to do their washing. Every day six or seven women could be seen at the washbasins.

Madame Colignone told Fred that her house had belonged to her mother, that she was born there as well as married there. It was a good guess that it was the same, except for the electric lights, as the day she was born. She also said that during the last war there were many American soldiers in the area. In fact, some used the same room as Fred.

★ ★ ★

Major Convery was introduced to a very high ranking officer that came to Wing Headquarters just to see how the procedures of the AA Early Warning was handled. He, of course, came to see General Barcus but Convery was called in. He came to see the way the operation was different from the other Armies. The system worked and worked well, whereas the Early Warning procedure of the other Armies did not seem to function very well. As a matter of fact, he said that when he was at the AA section of the 3rd Army, he was told that it couldn't be done because no one else was doing it. But we were doing it and had been since February and March. The 7th Army said that it worked and they liked it.

The officers of the AA section of the 7th Army told him that Convery had been behind the Early Warning all the way through France. When General Barcus told Fred who was coming, he also told him to be sure and be available, and not to go anywhere without letting him know. The Major was told that the General wanted to see him personally. The General was Major General Oldfield, AA advisor on the staff of General Arnold, who was the Commanding General of the Army Air Forces. As far as the AA was concerned, with the Air Forces, *there just wasn't anybody higher than General Oldfield.*

★ ★ ★

Fred didn't have any place to go and couldn't have gone if he had wanted to because his jeep was on a two-day trip with another officer. He did go down to his quarters and got ready to clean some clothes. He had mentioned to his driver that he needed some high test gas to do some cleaning, and in some manner or other a couple of gallons showed up. Where his driver got it and how, he did not know and did not ask any questions. He had used it before. It was wonderful stuff for cleaning, but in cold weather it was awful. It froze your fingers in no time at all. He called up Doc Archers of the medical detachment and asked him whether he had any rubber gloves. He said that he had some in a gas kit that would not be affected by gasoline and that they could be had. With Captain Archer offering gloves, Fred offered some of his gasoline for cleaning. He came down to Fred's quarters and they both cleaned some clothes. The gloves helped. In order to keep from freezing their fingers, it was still necessary to put on wool gloves inside the rubber gloves. That worked well and they were able to clean several sets of shirts and slacks.

★ ★ ★

The jeep was winterized to make it a bit more comfortable. Riding in an open jeep in freezing weather was terrible. Now it was closed in with plywood. It had some rather large cracks where the plywood joined the body and windshield, but nevertheless it kept out the mud and wind. The winter of 1944-45 was bitterly cold and riding in a jeep was real torture. Army boundaries were changed and the Wing Headquarters came into the 3rd Army jurisdiction, commanded by General Patton. Immediately, orders came down that all jeeps would have no improvised additions, which meant that we rode in the open.

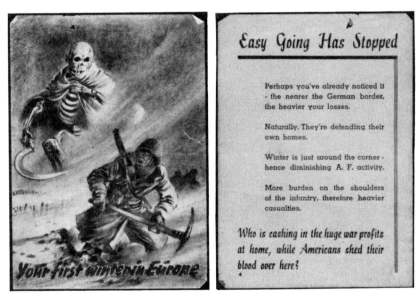

Easy Going Has Stopped

Perhaps you've already noticed it - the nearer the German border, the heavier your losses.

Naturally. They're defending their own homes.

Winter is just around the corner - hence diminishing A. F. activity.

More burden on the shoulders of the infantry, therefore heavier casualties.

Who is cashing in the huge war profits at home, while Americans shed their blood over here?

Flyer that was dropped over American lines during the winter of 1944

One December day an officer came in to see about some problems and stayed for supper. He brought along an excellent souvenir. It was a knife carried by German storm troopers that was given to them when they graduated from the Storm Trooper school. It was quite a knife, about 8 inches long, engraved, and in a scabbard. The officer got it from a warehouse at Savern the day after Savern was captured. He picked up enough for all of the officers of his group Headquarters and several extras. His colonel was an officer in Harry Truman's Battery during WWI. His colonel sent two to President Truman. Just to give you an idea of the way GIs prize such a souvenir, his driver got hold of several extra and it was rumored that he sold them for $100.00 each. That was against regulations and probably was not done, but that was the rumor—rumors, by the way, were something we had plenty of. The knives were all brand new and had never been issued.

★ ★ ★

Marcelle and some of her little girlfriends between the ages of ten and twelve were playing some sort of a game. Just for fun, Fred got out some popcorn, his gasoline Coleman stove, and got ready to pop some of the corn Esta had sent. They had never seen popcorn before. He told them that he was a magician and would make the corn turn into snow by using the heat of the stove. To pop the corn he used that coffee pot he carried along. It really worked because it had a handle that was easy to hold. It was made of aluminum and the lid kept the corn from popping out.

About the time the corn began to get hot and ready to pop, he told each one to speak into the pot and say *Hocus-Pocus*. Hocus-Pocus, spoken with a French accent by excited little girls, was something he'd never forget. Then, as the corn popped, he said, "Hocus-Pocus Alley Oop." *Alley Oop* in French means *to go up*. Then the laughter, with both amusement and surprise as they said the magic words and the corn popped, would have warmed anybody's heart. When the corn was put into a bowl and they tasted it, it disappeared with the same magic as it had appeared. However, at first, when the corn was popping, he did not have the lid on and they started scrambling for the kernels popping out of the pot.

★ ★ ★

Newspaper clipping from *Stars & Stripes Weekly*:
"ANY COMBAT SOLDIER"
He can hike 60 miles,
And then run five at that;
He could do the obstacle course
In nothing flat.
He digs slit trenches quicker
Than three men combined,
But Jones is no soldier—
His shoes are not shined.
Private Jones never goldbricks
He's a glutton for work,
But he holds no rating
Like the company clerk.
He keeps up morale
With songs that are gay.
But Jones is no soldier—
He needs a shave today.
With a rifle he's an expert—
Never misses a shot.
And he's cool as an iceberg
When the action is hot.
He's killed 50 Jerries,
And wounded 20 to boot
But Jones is no soldier—
He forgets to salute.
With a grenade, he is deadly,
Also with bayonet.
And out on patrol
He's the best I've seen yet.
As a scout he's uncanny,
Never known to guess wrong,
But Jones is no soldier—

His hair is too long.
If I am ever in trouble,
And I need help real quick;
If I'm cut off from my outfit,
And the Jerries are thick;
If the mortars are falling,
Like a lot of hailstones,
Well—the hell with all the soldiers,
Send me Private Jones.

—T-5 Carl D. Westerberg

★ ★ ★

It was January of 1945 and the morning was going along with its usual rush of grief and getting things straightened out. There were several long phone calls made and it was a rather trying morning. Fred had just gone downstairs to lunch and was starting to enjoy a bowl of good turkey soup when all hell broke loose with a hell of an explosion. Glass flew in every direction, along with a roar. He was picked up and tossed about twenty feet. Of course, everybody thought they were being bombed, and everyone started running for a ditch outside the building. On the way out, Fred noticed several of the men from the second floor dropping out of the windows. No one knew definitely what had happened and they all expected another explosion at almost any minute. But there were no planes in the air. People—civilians, youngsters, soldiers, officers, waitresses—began appearing, cut up and bleeding from flying glass.

As Defense Officer, Fred went down in the village looking for some strange men who had been reported a short time before, thinking they might have had something to do with it. All the people were out in the street wondering what had happened. A lieutenant came up and asked where he could get some trucks or vehicles. He said he was certain a number of his men had been injured, but he did not know for sure. He said that a TNT dump had gone up a short distance away. The Major was positive then that the strange men had something to do with it, so he grabbed a couple of soldiers, located the men, and took them to Headquarters, where they were turned over to some other guards to be held for questioning. They were held all afternoon and then finally turned loose because they were okay.

What caused the TNT to go up, no one knew. One truck had been loaded, another was standing by waiting to be loaded, and a jeep drove in beside one of the trucks. That's all anyone knew. (They found this out later when Major Bunn, Major Murtland, and Major Convery went over to investigate.) Two trucks, one jeep, and nine men just disappeared. They found parts of everything scattered all over the field. The dump was about a quarter of a mile in a straight line from the Control Room.

Each one of the nine craters created by the explosion of the nine piles of TNT was approximately 25 feet in diameter and about 15 to 20 feet deep. All nine let go at once. The detail had come to move the TNT to some other place.

The TNT had been stockpiled in a field about a quarter of a mile away to be used on the Fortress Metz, located about 40 miles away from the field where the TNT had been brought and stored for a special purpose. The fortress had been surrounded but could not be taken. It was possible for the troops to crawl all over the fortress, but it was impossible to get the Germans out. TNT had been brought in with the idea of dropping it down through ventilating pipes and blasting out whatever Germans were in the fortress. However, they surrendered before that was necessary. The TNT was not used.

TNT becomes very unstable when it has been repeatedly frozen and then thawed. Because the temperature had been freezing at night and warming during the day, the weather was the reason for the explosion.

Every window in the Headquarters building they were using and, in fact, the windows of every house and building in the village were broken. Doors and shutters were blown off. It blew some people clear across rooms, but very few were badly injured. However, Captain Archers, the medical officer, said he and his aides treated about 150 persons for cuts. One officer had a piece right in his temple that cut an artery, but he was not badly hurt. One woman got a knock on the head and probably had a concussion.

The window of Fred's room was completely blown out and the back wall of the building was loose from the rest of the house. He was only there for a few minutes to find out whether Madame Colignone and Marcelle were okay. They were not injured at all.

The Headquarters building was ruined. It was actually declared by the engineers to be unfit for further use. The roof was loose and all of the tiles were loosened by the blast. The roof practically lifted up and then dropped down again. It looked like the war came to them rather than their going to war. Fred's only injury came from two small pieces of glass—one hit his cheek and the other his chin. He didn't bleed anymore than he would have if he had nicked himself while shaving.

The whole Headquarters had to move to a new location. It did not have to be condemned to get people to move. As long as the weather stayed cold, it would have been all right as far as the roof was concerned, but as soon as the snow melted and it started to rain, the roof would not have been able to keep out the water. With all the windows boarded up, it just was not satisfactory.

★ ★ ★

When Headquarters moved to Nancy after the building was ruined by the explosion, space was obtained on the second floor of a large office building. The building was the head office of a steel mill and was quite adequate. Only a part of the building was used. The rest of the building was still in use by the steel company.

One thing about that modern building that was surprising was the restroom that was designed to be used by both sexes. The room was quite large, about thirty feet by fifteen. Along the left wall were the urinals for the men. On the right side were the women's urinals (not as many). These were drain holes in the floor. The hole was in the center of a three foot square that sloped toward the hole. In front of the hole were footprints in the concrete, apparently for the purpose of proper aim. Farther back along the right wall were several normal toilet compartments.

Convery's new quarters were in a hotel that the Wing had taken over for the officers. It worked out to be a good deal. Being a Major, he had a room to himself with a private bath on the fifth floor, which was the top floor. He had to go to the top floor in order to get a bath because the ranks higher than his started on the second floor. In France, the second floor was named the first and the first was named the ground floor. The bath had a nice big tub and a double washbasin. The Wing also arranged to take over all of the employees of the hotel, including dining room and kitchen personnel. Regular rations were drawn and turned over to the employees for cooking.

★ ★ ★

Quite a bit has been said about the Operations Room and how it controlled the aircraft from the ground. It took a little while to get used to the language used because there were many words that were more or less code but not actually secret. One word took the place of a sentence and saved a lot of time. For example, the controller might have said to a pilot over the radio, "Heads up!" He meant, "Look out because there are hostile aircraft in the area that have more altitude than you do." Of course, that was very bad. A *bandit* was a hostile aircraft, and a *bogie* was an aircraft that no one knew whether was friendly or hostile. *Angels* were *thousands of feet in altitude. Angels 10* meant *10,000 feet.*

The controller had a crew of men under him who could tell exactly where an aircraft was just by listening to the pilot transmit for a fix using a direction finder. One day a pilot returned from over the lines where he had been hit by flack (AA fire) and had one wing afire. He bailed out, and within 15 minutes the controller had an ambulance there to pick him up.

Of course, every radio, every telephone, and every unit had a code name, so when one listened to what was going on, it just didn't make sense if you hadn't been around the Ops Room.

★ ★ ★

Newspaper clipping from *Stars & Stripes Weekly*:
"TRY THIS ON YOUR PIANO"
Like *Mademoiselle from Armentiers*, or any other soldier song, the words of *The Bucharest Cannonball*, official song of the interned Allied airmen in Bucharest, cannot be traced to any one man.

You can't find agreement, even on who started the thing which, like Topsy, just grew into a multi-versed almost endless thing. And for some of the verses, you'll have to get a personal audience with any of 1,000-odd men who remember them—they can't be published in a family newspaper.

The tune was a straight steal from *The Wabash Cannonball*, but from there on all similarity ends. To give you an idea:
Across the Adriatic through spacious skies of blue,
There came a thousand bombers, with airmen tried and true.
They headed for the Balkans, and straight for Bucharest,
But when they reached Flak Valley, the gunners did the rest.
They all landed safely, with parachutes galore,
And now we're in a prison camp asweatin' out the war.

★ ★ ★

The German Air Force seemed to be deteriorating, and the AA problems were getting easier all the time. However, everything had to be kept going just the same as before.

★ ★ ★

Two officers came in from the front and brought along two Red Cross girls who were on their way to Paris where they were to be transferred. The girls had endured a long cold ride, so Fred offered them his room in which to tidy up. Civilians were not allowed beyond the first floor but military personnel were okay. He fixed some drinks for them all. The girls made good use of the bathroom. They had been able to have hot showers but no hot baths for a long time and they really appreciated the luxury. Afterward they all went to dinner. The meal and service really made a hit. The girls stayed at a transient hotel for military personnel traveling on orders. Fred arranged for the officers to stay at the hotel. In the morning the officers told him that the girls thought he was tops. He didn't do a thing but hand them towels. Nevertheless, they gave him credit for it all. You know how they felt. When one was nearly always cold, had to keep near a fire to get warm, things were not clean, and food was not nicely served, the change to what we were now fortunate enough to have was something that made quite an impression.

It was not known how long the hotel could be used. It might have to be given up anytime. But while there, it certainly was enjoyed. Street cars were running again. In the morning they would wake everybody up as they crossed some tracks below. Whoever would have thought they would be fighting a war that way!

★ ★ ★

When they first moved into the hotel, the front was not too far away, and everything was being done in a military wartime fashion. About that time, Germany was being heavily bombed. Many flights were passing overhead on the way to Germany and, of course, on the way back to England. Quite often the bombers would be damaged from ack-ack fire while over Germany and sometimes could not get back to England, forcing them to land somewhere in France.

The 64th Fighter Wing tried several times to get the frequencies and crystals necessary to monitor the bomber radio talk and help in any way possible. Apparently, the Fighter Command and the Bomber Command did not understand one another because it was impossible to obtain the necessary crystals. Several bombers crash landed on their way back to England. Personnel from the Fighter Wing went to the planes, obtained the radios and crystals, took them back to the Wing and set radios to monitor the planes as they came back. A number of damaged planes were contacted and brought in safely to airfields under the 64th Fighter Wing. The pilots were really grateful.

One memorable day in Nancy, Major Convery was leaving a barber shop and met Captain Olsen, who said he had been looking all over for him as he was wanted at Headquarters. There was going to be a ceremony and Convery was to receive a Bronze Star. Fred dashed up to Headquarters and got there just twenty minutes before the ceremony. All who were to be there from outlying installations had been notified, but the sergeant forgot to tell the people close by. Anyway it all went off smoothly and Major Convery, along with about twenty-five others, were decorated with the Bronze Star. His decoration was for the planning and work that he did on the Early Warning setup for AA artillery during the invasion of Southern France.

The chaplain told a story he had recently heard. All of the GIs knew a few words of French, such as *bon* which meant *good*, and had some idea of French pronunciation. One GI was trying to trade some soap for some eggs with a French woman. He wanted to say that the soap was good for her face. So he said, *"Bon for your face,"* meaning *"Good for your face,"* and used a French accent to pronounce *face* like *faas*. Now, the correct French for *face* was *visage*, and the word *faas* meant *ass*. Can you imagine what she thought? At first she didn't know what he meant, but when he started to wipe his face, she understood and began laughing. Most of the time sign language could be used to get by, with a few words of French.

★ ★ ★

In 1945, zippers had only been in use about three or four years and were not the quality of the zippers we now have. The zipper on Fred's OD pants wore out and the metal part pulled away from the cloth strip. He took the trousers to a *taileur*, but nothing could be done about it because he didn't have any zippers. He then got a zipper from an officer who had picked up some in Paris for his pants. It worked okay for a couple of days until one afternoon when he came into the hotel and went to his room. The power was off so he had to walk up five flights of stairs. He went to the bathroom, cleaned up, and then went down to lunch, turning his key in at the desk. He went into the dining room and, glancing downward, noticed that he was wide open. He turned in a hurry to close the zipper because there were two Red Cross girls at one of the tables nearby. But the damn thing had come off the wrong end and he couldn't do a thing with it. He stepped out into the hallway and then to the water closet for *messieurs* and tried to fix it. No luck. The only thing to do was to hike back up to his room and change. When he got up there, he found that he had not picked up his key from the desk. He had to hike back down, get the key, hike back up, and then change. (Remember that he was on the fifth floor.) He was sure disgusted with French zippers. Back in Africa he had to have buttons put on his "pinks" (the slang term for dress slacks) because the zipper went haywire. He probably would have to do the same thing with his ODs.

★ ★ ★

February began with beautiful days and the whole sky being clear. The first day of clear weather everywhere meant all the fighter bombers went to work. For a long time they had to work between breaks in the weather and very often there would be a lot of grief getting them back to their bases. Sometimes they would go up with the weather clear. Then when they came back, the weather had closed in and they only had enough gas to stooge around for about half an hour. If they did not get in somewhere, they ran out of gas and the pilot had to either bail out or belly in. With the better weather, everything was up. The planes were going out, finding their target, and then coming back for another mission, only staying on the field for about an hour while they were gassed and bombed up. On those good days more planes were up than ever before. Days like that were CAVU meaning Ceiling and Visibility Unlimited.

★ ★ ★

Nearly all of the German forces were on the run. A flight of fighter bombers caught a column of German trucks without proper air-cover. They bombed up and down the column until they were out of bombs and had to return to their bases. Before they returned, they dropped their spare gas tanks on the column rather than return with the gas. The gas tank would break open upon hitting and catch fire, thereby acting like a bomb on anything it happened to hit.

★ ★ ★

One of the controllers reported that one of our flights was in a dogfight with a group of Jerry planes over a Jerry airfield. The Jerries wanted to quit because they were running out of gas but our flight wouldn't let them. Final result: two destroyed and a couple damaged.

★ ★ ★

Foo Fire was something that the fighter pilots talked about, swore that it was actual, but nobody knew just exactly what it was. In talking to night-fighter pilots several times, they were positive that the stuff was there. At first, people just laughed at them and made all kinds of remarks, but when other officers came back from missions and reported seeing the *Foo Fire*, it began to be something to consider. The pilots reported that the stuff would follow along with them a short distance off their wing tips. It even turned when they did and they couldn't get away from it.

It looked like a ball of fire. It was screwy and really got on their nerves. A night-fighter pilot, flying on instruments only, for hours at a time, knowing only where he was by radio contacts and instruments, with no lights of any kind on or in the plane, is strained most of the time. Something like *Foo Fire* would give the jitters to anyone. The night-fighter pilots had a rough tough assignment. The night fighters were used over enemy territory to shoot out any lights that they might see.

★ ★ ★

Many times when the fighter bombers would go their maximum distance into enemy territory they would be late in getting back to their airfield. If there were any delays, many times the darkness would close in and they could not find their base. Bear in mind that the airfields were not the same as our airfields of today. There were no runway lights and, for security reasons, no other lights of any kind. Everything had to be blacked out. Consequently, getting a plane in at night was extremely difficult. It was always the plan for planes to come back before dark. On one occasion there were several planes in a flight coming back and darkness had closed in. The controller, by talking to the pilots, knew where they were and could guide them to their airfields. With no lighting of any kind, it was impossible for the pilots to locate their base. The controller then called the airfield and told them to put up their *candle*. At each airfield there would be an old-time searchlight that had been used during the early days of the war for locating enemy planes at night. Their use for that purpose had been discontinued. Putting up the candle meant that the searchlight was pointed straight up, giving the pilots a point to head for. On one occasion, it was very late and very dark. The controller ordered all trucks that were anywhere near the airfield to get lined up on either side of the landing strip and turn on their headlights. This gave the pilots light enough to see where they were to land. Actually they all landed safely. There were some anxious moments because some of the planes were running low on gas and it was all they could do to reach the field.

★ ★ ★

Newspaper clipping from *Stars & Stripes Weekly*:
"FRONT-LINE FLASHES"

Some Krauts facing the 5th Army beachhead forces believe in being prepared for the worst. It's a source of constant amazement to the Americans, who at best have only khaki issue handkerchiefs, where the enemy gets all the material he uses for surrendering. Generally it's a bed sack substitute for the white flag. Other Krauts play them closer. They have little white pennants with small—very—black swastikas.

★ ★ ★

Major Convery was in an Alsace-Loraine area shortly after the American forces had taken it over. From the second floor windows, white sheets or flags would be hanging out. A few days later when he came through the area, the houses all had American flags hanging from the windows. He found out that every home had three flags—German, white, and American. Possession of the area had changed hands several times, so, depending on which of the forces held the town, the townspeople would choose the appropriate flag. White was used if the fighting was close.

★ ★ ★

A day came along when it seemed to be right but everything that went on had something wrong with it. That evening several, for a change, decided to go out for dinner. Army grub was good, but one did get tired of it once in awhile. They matched to see who would pay for whom and Fred lost. He had to take an officer by the name of Long. The meal consisted of thin soup, so dark that it looked like bouillon but tasted like water that had been used to wash out a gravy bowl; plain bread, dark, no butter; a piece of fish the size of a small salmon steak. They had raw vegetables, turnips, carrots, a little potato, and something that looked like and chewed like asparagus—but they were without salt and pepper. Then they had watery mashed potatoes with gravy over them that probably was the same soup they were served—but hadn't finished. No coffee, but they did have a bottle of real cheap wine. Dessert was a bit of small, wrinkled, and dried-up apple. Fred paid the bill, and for the two of them it was 320 francs, $6.20. He tipped the waiter, and the better part of $7.00 was gone. The place didn't add anything toward the cost either, because it was crowded and not too clean. Pepper was spilled on the tables. When he walked out, he put his hand in his (short . coat) pocket and his camera was gone. That really kept him mad for a long time. The weather was getting good and he was planning to take a lot of pictures. They went back to the hotel. He got in a poker game and lost 1500 francs.

★ ★ ★

Back in a pilot's training days when he was at his training station, pilots were allowed to take up the fighter planes to get in their hours. One pilot who had just recently been married took his bride along. Wanting to have some fun and give her an exciting time, he did some aerial acrobatics with the plane and scared the poor girl to death. Loops and turns, etc. were not particularly to her liking. As they were doing this, she would say, "Tommy, stop" and then again, "Tommy, stop." She did this several times, and then over the radio telephone came the voice of an officer, monitoring the radio transmissions from the open mike. He called the flight by its number and said, "You are breaking radio silence. This is against regulations. You will not transmit unless you have a definite message."

A little while later the pilot continued to do his rolls and loops and forgot also that the mike switch was open. His bride again complained quite emphatically for him to stop, saying, "Tommy, if you don't quit this, I'll wet my pants." This remark was heard over the radio telephone and the message came back, "Madam, you will observe radio silence. We are not in the least bit concerned with the condition of your underwear."

★ ★ ★

Along this same line there was another incident similar in nature. The letters of the alphabet were all designated by various names. For example A was Able, B was Baker, C was Charlie, D was Dog, F was Fox, etc. The reply to a message, when received, was to give Roger for the letter R.

A flight was on its way and the leader of the flight was carrying on instructions to the other pilots. One of the pilots came back, after receiving a message, with the reply, *"Roger-Dodger,"* a slang expression frequently used. The flight leader called the pilot and said, "You will not use *Roger-Dodger,* just the code *Roger."* Things went on for awhile, and a little later another message was put out and the pilot came back with *Roger-Dodger.* This irritated the flight commander who replied to the pilot, "You will not use *Roger-Dodger.* I am a Major, and that is an order." The pilot who had committed the sin said over the radio telephone, *"Roger-Dodger,* you old codger, I'm a Major too."

★ ★ ★

One particular morning was important and very busy. A full Colonel from the AA section of the 7th Army came, accompanied by another full Colonel, a Lieutenant Colonel, and a Captain from Supreme Headquarters of U.S. forces in Europe. The 7th Army was quite proud of our arrangements for Early Warning. They thought it was the best. The previously- mentioned group had been at Army Headquarters learning all about that end of things and were well impressed. Once again they came to visit our operations, not with the idea of criticizing, but with the idea of finding out what we did. Actually, they had been to all of the Armies for the same purpose. The Colonel from 7th Army AA section said that what we had was the ideal combination—rather a nice thing for the AA officer of 7th Army to say in front of the Colonel from Supreme Headquarters of U.S. forces in Europe.

Col. Nelson B. Jackson, CO of 64th Fighter Wing.
Major Convery in back row on the right.

★ ★ ★

The rate of exchange of money when the Germans occupied France was 20 francs for one mark. That gave the Germans all kinds of money to buy anything. They bought supplies (personal use) on the black market which made things worse with every purchase. They bought all kinds of things and sent them back to Germany. The result was that stocks were bought up entirely, prices went sky high, and the value of the franc went way down. When the U.S. troops arrived, there was nothing to buy, prices were even higher, and two cents had to be paid for every franc.

PART V

GERMANY

Near Worms

March 1945

23 March 1945 . . . What a day that was! All of the AA units were moving along with everything else. We were not moving, but what a lot of work it was trying to keep in touch by any means possible. AA units wanted connections they couldn't have and wanted things done that couldn't be done. In other words, work was getting crazier by the hour. Fred felt like he was being run through a wringer. The big push was on, and crossings were being made of the Rhine.

Convery was getting ready for his first trip into Germany that was to last for three or four days. He went to the hotel to get his stuff to take along. The C & R (Command and Recon) car was parked in front of the hotel, and his driver went in to get his sleeping bag and some emergency rations. He came out to load up and the C & R was gone. The MPs had picked it up because there was no driver with it. That meant that they had to hike about a mile to the MP station and get it out of hock.

Convery had no idea that things were starting out wrong, but they got the car and began the trip. On the way, a shaft in the top broke, so they pulled into an emergency ordinance shop and had that fixed. While the mechanic was working, they had some lunch and then started out again.

Just as they were about to pass a two-and-a-half-ton truck, it swerved clear over to the left-hand side for no reason whatsoever. The truck forced them into a tree beside the road. Trees were all along the side of the highway and quite close to the road. If they drove on the shoulder at all, there was about two or three feet before coming to the row of trees. They hit a tree with the left front wheel, breaking the spring loose from the axle and putting a hole in the oil pan.

Fred hitched a ride into the next town, leaving his driver with the recon and looked up an ordinance outfit. They came out and looked over the car. The wrecker was out on a trip, and they could not come at that time. While he was waiting, the Captain of the ordinance unit came and told him that they had a recon that he could borrow while they repaired his. The Ordinance Company was just for the purpose of repairing vehicles. Fred waited in the Captain's office and visited with him while they sent for his driver. They sent a guard along and said they would pick up the car when the wrecker returned. When Fred's driver arrived, he transferred their stuff to the other car. They were off and didn't get back to Headquarters for several days.

★ ★ ★

They went up into Germany, drove all over the area that the Army was in at that time, located the place where the new Headquarters was to be, and then returned.

Fred returned to Nancy for two days and then went back into Germany where Headquarters was to be stationed in a large building that had previously been used as a girls' music college. Prior to that, the building had been the summer home of a German prince. The building was about 200 feet square with a courtyard in the center and was two stories high.

On the trip, which lasted five days, he really covered miles and miles. He went through the Siegfried line as well as the Maginot line. Those rows and rows of concrete dragon teeth certainly made a person wonder how anyone could ever get through them, particularly with all of them covered by heavy guns.

* * *

Siegfried Line

Some of the larger towns he went through were Kaiserlautern and Worms. On the other side of the Rhine, he was in Mannheim. The Rhine crossing was on a pontoon bridge that had just been put in by the engineers. He saw quite a number of released Polish and Russian prisoners on their way back home, also a great number of people who had been doing the so-called slave labor and had been released upon the advance of the Armies. Whenever prisoners or slave laborers were released, they were just turned loose and were on their own to get back to their homes the best way they could.

The people of Germany were quite a bit different from those of France. The women were all quite a bit broader in the beam and more buxom. The men looked typically German, wearing visor caps and boots, whereas the French wore long trousers and berets. There were very few people in the towns. As they drove through the streets, those who were about looked at them with no expression at all. They had been getting smiles and waves in other areas but none in Germany.

★ ★ ★

Fred really felt rather foolish once when he asked someone when Easter was going to be and was told that Easter had been the previous Sunday. That showed that he had no idea of time anymore.

★ ★ ★

Most of the people had left the towns, and the towns were practically deserted, with only a few people here and there. Most were just poking around in the rubble looking for something that might be of value and trying to find anything that might be left of their homes. One thing was certain and that was that the German people did want to have things clean. He went through one town that was totally different from the way it had looked when he had gone through a few days before. The first time, the streets and sidewalks were dirty with rubble and broken glass that had been left after a bulldozer had cleared the streets for traffic. The bulldozers cleared away the debris in the same manner as if they were clearing a road or street for traffic after a heavy snowfall. When he went through the second time, people were sweeping the streets and sidewalks in front of the homes that were still livable.

Fred heard that German people were supposed to be clean about their homes, but he had been told that the German women were not clean personally. It didn't make any difference to him because he could not talk to any of them except on official business. The regulation was *No one will fraternize*. That meant that they could not associate with them in any way. He was beginning to get along fairly well with the French language he had picked up, but he did not expect he would ever have to speak German.

It was not expected he was to be quartered with any families.

★ ★ ★

Headquarters did not have any German employees around at all. They did have a few Polish girls to wait on the officers' mess and do the KP work in the kitchen. They were some of those who had been released from doing the work on railroads. They were tickled to death to be working for us and were quite amusing. When they first came to work, they all wore light trousers. They were given dresses taken from a house that had been confiscated for military purposes. It made them quite happy. They were robust girls, being like German women, heavy busted and broad beamed. They probably got that way from working on the railroads which they did for twelve to fourteen hours a day. All they had to eat was mostly soup and potatoes.

Once several of them were found crying together. One of the soldiers who spoke Polish asked what was wrong. They thought the Americans did not like the way they had been working. They wanted so much to please and felt bad because they thought they were not doing right. It turned out that the mess sergeant had told them to quit working at 4:30 and take some time off. They had been going all day long, like beavers, getting things cleaned out and straightened in the kitchen. They only understood working from early in the morning until late at night without a stop and thought they had displeased us. They really did a good job. They almost ran between the kitchen and dining room.

★ ★ ★

Headquarters was located on the French side of the Rhine, looking out over the Rhine Valley. A rather interesting thing happened. While in radio communications with another Headquarters about 100 miles north, the words would be cut off entirely. Other times the transmissions would be clear as a bell, with no breaks. It would happen right in the middle of a conversation. Everything would be going along fine, and then the words just quit. Finally it was figured out. It was a straight line between the two stations, and the flights of bombers coming over from England, on their way to Germany on bombing runs, would be passing through the radio beam. Each plane, as it passed, would stop the radio transmissions for an instant. The same thing would happen when the flights were returning.

★ ★ ★

One day shortly after they arrived at the building that had been used as a music school, Fred went down to where the enlisted men had been billeted in a building that had been the servants' quarters when the building had been the summer quarters for a German prince. The power generators had not yet been wired into the building, so there were no lights. Scattered around the halls were a number of kerosene lamps set in wall brackets. Some GI who apparently did not know the difference between gasoline and kerosene had filled one of the lamps with gasoline and lit the wick. The gasoline had become warm, expanded, ran over, and was burning outside of the lamp. It was making quite a flame. About ten GIs were standing around looking at it, not knowing what to do. Fred took the lamp, went to the doorway, and threw it as far as he could. It, of course, broke and made a ball of fire when it landed. It was rather foolish on his part but it turned out okay. He didn't get burned and neither did the building.

★ ★ ★

Tile stove

The rooms in the building all faced inward toward the court. Around the rooms ran a hall. The rooms were heated by huge tile stoves almost six feet high. Each stove consisted of several separate chambers, each above the other, with a smoke-way between. The stoves were against the hallway wall, with the firebox opening in the hallway. With this arrangement the stoves could be kept going without the servants coming into the rooms.

* * *

The war was going along fast. Once again we were way behind the lines and were as far behind as we were the week before even though we had moved up about 150 miles. We had to act and do things quite a bit differently than we did before. We could not be nearly as free as we had been in our movements. Going ahead that fast, we knew that there were still a lot of Jerries left behind in the hills and woods. Some were to be concerned about and others were not. We never knew which were which and had to treat them all alike.

* * *

Fred made a trip to Darmstadt, a fairly large town, that was ruined except for its outer edge. The RAF only hit the town once, but it had been bombed for forty minutes at that time. The cities were more concentrated than ours, with no spaces between the buildings at all. If you could imagine a pile of rubble about the size of the business district of Tacoma, Washington, you would have some idea of what it was like.

* * *

It was April and Fred had been soldiering for over four years. The end appeared to be a long way off. Of course, it was the one thing that everyone thought and dreamed about. They dreamed of the old days, but although they were actually several years older, the war had added additional years of a different kind onto our lives. When he read over letters Esta had sent on from other people, the things they wrote about were sort of penny-ante, little and frivolous. He wondered if the things that bothered people at home would trouble him when he got back. Would he be the sort of person who would be bothered by nothing and would not care what happened? Would life and all the problems of living, the details of getting along with other people, seem important enough to be done properly? Or would the old civilian life, which now

218

seemed to be Utopia, turn out to be something more or less child-ish in comparison to his present method of living, with its excite-ment and at the same time serious responsibility?

★ ★ ★

All through the war and up to April of 1945 Fred had not been actually in the front line. He had been in places a number of times that were not healthy, but it had not been necessary for him to live in a foxhole. However, he was in daily contact with the war and all that went with it. Planes were shot down and it did not mean anything other than another figure on reports. The reports listed the losses with the remark MIA (missing in action) or pilot bailed safely. The point is that those were things they were dealing with every day. If a truck was wrecked—that is, not seriously—it would be repaired if possible, and if not, it went into an ordinance shop. If they could not repair it, they could get an-other. There were no personal losses of any kind. They ate and slept. The only problem of living was staying alive. The problems of living a civilian life would be dull and monotonous.

★ ★ ★

All the rooms on both floors of the building in which they were living were almost thirty feet to the ceiling and about thirty feet square. All furnishings had been left in place, and some, in fact most of them, were beautiful. They had to move everything out in order to use the rooms, and soon the rooms lost all of their glamour. Furniture piled in a corner was anything but beautiful. There were quite a few large paintings of various people who lived in the building in years past. There must have been a large num-ber of servants because in the basement there were a number of rooms for servants. One room was full of barrels of stored dinner-ware, none of which was very good. Beds were all over the place. There were even a half dozen grand pianos. In the basement was stored a large amount of wine in wine casks—some of it was pretty good. They used quite a bit of the furniture fixing up the of-fices, and of course the beds were needed.

One piece of the German prince's furniture was a souvenir that Fred would really liked to have sent home but he was out-ranked. It was a two-foot-square box-like looking piece made of inlaid wood. It had four legs like a table. The upper four inches was a hinged lid. When the lid was lifted up, a leather-covered seat appeared with a toilet-sized opening under which was a chamber pot. What a conversation piece that would have been. Closed up, it really looked like some sort of end table.

★ ★ ★

They were not to fraternize in any way with the German people, which certainly limited them. And the country was not as friendly as Italy and France. One could hardly expect it. As Fred went through those large towns, he had a certain amount of sym-pathy. But, when he saw the women and older men hauling carts of belongings, broken up lumber for fuel, etc., he generally thought, "It's too bad, but you asked for it."

★ ★ ★

On a trip into the Heidelberg area, they were heading up the autobahn (same as our freeways). They were traveling along at a good speed with no problems whatsoever. It was wonderful to be out on a real highway. They came to a place that looked like there had not been much travel at all. In fact, branches of trees and leaves were scattered on the highway. They slowed up a little bit because something was wrong. It was fortunate that they did, because they came to the end of the autobahn—the end was where a bridge had been. Had they been going too fast or had it been dark, they would have taken right off into the river.

The bridge was a high crossing over the river into Heidelberg which was quite a city. It was not an industrial town and very pic-turesque. Consequently, it had not been hit badly and seemed to be in pretty good shape.

★ ★ ★

You could certainly see the preponderance of women over men. People were beginning to come back into the fields. Two weeks before, the fields did not look like they had been worked at all but now were beginning to show some care. Most of those working in the fields were women, children, and old men. Here and there were a few younger men. Probably they were "self-discharged" from the German Army. Every so often all the men were rounded up and checked.

★ ★ ★

During eight days, the Major was in the towns of Nancy in France, Worms, Darmstadt, Auffanburg, and Nuremberg in Germany. At Nuremberg, there was still fighting in the city.

There is not much to say about the towns and cities that he passed through. All were the same—just piles of rubble with passageways cleared through by military bulldozers to make way for traffic. Maybe he was taking part in the start or end of history that would last forever. He thought that the First World War had been forgotten, but how this war would ever be forgotten was beyond him.

The kind of rubble told the type of bombs that were used. If the bombs were explosive, halves of buildings would be left, with the rooms open for everyone to look into. If the bombs were incendiary, only the walls would be left, with all of the interior masonry dropped down inside. Explosive bombs piled the rubble up outside.

One city of 300- to 400,000 people had not been touched, with the exception of the railroad yards. There were quite a number of German troops there when the Army advanced. The German troops were given 48 hours to evacuate, and when they did not leave, the town was bombed. Then there was nothing.

★ ★ ★

The roads in Germany were far better than those in France, but they could not be used all the time because so often the bridges would be out. Long detours had to be made to get to where we wanted to go. In planning a trip, you never figured mileage. It was all a matter of time. One place to another was just a number of hours because there were so many bridges destroyed. There were many things that entered into the time. Seldom could you ever drive straight through. If the main highway was out, you had to take the side highways and drive through every village. Each village would be a bottleneck, unless the village had two streets. Many times there would be either a cow-cart or maybe a push-cart in the middle of the street and you just had to wait until it got out of the way. Other times it would be a convoy of huge semi-freight trucks, trying to get around a sharp corner. One morning it took an hour and a quarter to make three miles.

* * *

Fred was happy to have a jeep for his travels rather than a big recon car. He came to one place not on the regular route. The bridge was over a river and the part that was blown was over land. In order to get to the other bank, dirt had been piled up at the end (a little bit). The railings had been torn off the sides of the bridge and laid down on the dirt for traction. The angle was at least 90 degrees. He had to wait for a captured civilian car to go first. When it started down, it hung up on the edge of the pavement where the bridge had dropped away. It couldn't go ahead and it couldn't back up. It was resting right on the drive shaft. There were some GIs there and they just picked up the back end and let it roll down. The jeep didn't have any trouble at all. Fred came back the same way in order to save time, but when he got there, the dirt had sort of worked away from the top and the iron railing that had been laid for each track was bent and out of shape.

At the top there was about an eight-inch concrete slab straight up. To go up slow and over that slab of concrete was out of the question. If the grade could be hit straight on, it would have helped, but it had to be hit at a slant because the next pier was in the way. Anyway, the driver, Francis (and he was a good driver), put the jeep in underdrive, 4-wheel drive, and low, and then gave the jeep all that it could take. They hit the concrete, made two bounces, front and rear wheels, and were on top of the bridge. At that angle and those bounces, going over backward would not have been a surprise. It was the only way though, and if they had not been able to go across the river that way, they would have had to go about 75 miles out of the way. It was getting dark, and they had no desire to be driving alone, in that part of the world, after sundown.

In Munich, the Wing had established Forward Headquarters in the offices of a brewery that was still intact. The building was quite fortunate because it was located next to a hill, and none of the bombs had hit it. It was also off to one side of the city. When Fred returned to his Headquarters, he brought along a keg of draft beer. It so happened that the brewery had its own power plant, was complete within itself and still had its refrigeration plant working. He got the beer from the storage room, so it was good and cold. It was still cold when he got in about 8:30. The 100 liter keg was tapped in the office. Officers were coming in and out all evening to have some. He was dead tired and wanted to go to bed, but couldn't while everyone was coming in.

The Major had to see about some searchlights that were getting on their night fighters every night. He made arrangements to stop them and let them know that the night fighters were in the searchlight area. The lights blinded the pilots and made it difficult for them to navigate. That kind of situation killed pilots and cracked up planes. German night fighters were one of the reasons for black-out conditions.

One night, while on a trip, Fred had to make a phone call to an AA unit. To get a line to that unit he had to go up a road about two miles. That night, and just about every night, a Jerry night fighter was going up and down the road, shooting at any light or anything that he could see. Major Convery was in a brick building that was blacked out very well, so no one was worried about Jerry. He could be heard coming over every so often and they knew what he was doing. When Fred left the building, Jerry was just going by, heading west. Fred knew that he would not be back for several minutes. They took off in the jeep for some woods that were at the top of a hill where he could make his call. While he was making the phone call, Jerry came back. He could be seen opening up on the traffic on the road. Fred was glad he wasn't there. As soon as Jerry passed, they went back to the place they started from. It was sort of like waiting for a train to pass on the trestle before crossing on foot. They knew just about how long it would take him to come back and how long he would travel up the road before turning around. Fred's driver had just come over from the States about a month before and didn't like it one little bit and was rather worried. Even though Fred was positive they could make it, he felt rather naked out on the highway in the bright moonlight.

With the front advancing as fast as it was, Maj. Convery had a lot of trouble keeping in touch with the units for which he was responsible. He hoped it kept up because the war could not last if it did. There were reports that the prisoners were coming in by the thousands. While talking to one unit, they said the prisoners were coming in so fast that they could not be handled. A small detachment of about 20 men were working in their Ops Room and said there were about 500 prisoners outside just waiting to be taken care of. The prisoners were told to just start walking back toward the prisoner-of-war cages. They were actually just wandering around loose. The air was full of rumors about what was happening and, of course, there was all of the radio news. The Major was sure that in another week or ten days, everything would be practically over.

VE Day

April 27, 1945
THE WAR WAS OVER!

Major Convery had known about it for three days when it was announced over the BBC broadcast. He couldn't get excited. None of them could. They should have been ecstatic. Everybody should have been getting drunk, but they just gradually quit working. For some reason or other, Fred had a kind of let-down feeling. His end of things had certainly quit in a hurry.

The big question was, "Will we stay here in Germany or go back to the States for duty there or move over to the South Pacific?" All were wondering.

★ ★ ★

As Safety Officer, the Major had to start making trips to the various airfields under the command of the 64th Fighter Wing. One trip lasted three days and he saw quite a bit more of Germany. He went to Augsburg and Munich, plus a number of small towns. Near Munich, along the side of the highways, people were streaming back from liberated camps, both prison and concentration. The French were grabbing any kind of transportation they could to get back home. He saw several who had taken a farm tractor and hitched about three wagons to it, loaded up the wagons with countrymen and started out. There were thousands walking, and all were heading away from Germany.

★ ★ ★

Civilian control was a matter of concern when the area was being taken over by the Army because the German plan was to have the civilians act as saboteurs. The civilians were protected from being labeled as spies (anyone committing a hostile or warlike activity out of uniform was considered a spy and not treated as a soldier) by giving them armbands to wear. One arm band was black and red and had DEUTSCHER VOLKSSTURM WEHRMACHT printed on it. Another arm band was just red with a Swastika on a white circle. The people called the WEHRMACHT were to poison water and foods, to disrupt communications, and to kill military personnel whenever possible. It was the Major's duty to keep all units informed of the possibilities of this situation. It so happened that nothing happened and there was no real trouble with the civilians. However, the plan existed and it was never known for sure whether something might break out.

Civilians could cause trouble. At the beginning of the advance into Germany, a unit was passing through a village. A young man with a rifle stepped out of a crowd of people alongside the road and shot the driver of one of the vehicles. The driver of another vehicle saw what happened, swung his truck out of the traffic lane, running over and killing the man.

On two separate occasions, one of the travelers had dropped to the ground, either sick, hurt, or dead. Usually in a case of that kind, any place else in the world, all others would stop and help. But in that situation no one stopped, and no one except the apparent partner in the trek was doing anything.

★ ★ ★

In one German prisoner area there were 42,000 prisoners guarded only by a couple of tanks and two AA 50mm machine guns. Each guard unit was faced with its line of fire along a line acting as a fence. There was no enclosure whatsoever. They were just there en masse, all standing up to keep warm. So many prisoners had been taken during the few days that it was impossible to handle them all. German soldiers who surrendered and who were not taken prisoner were given passes and turned loose to get back to their homes as best they could. The Army just did not want them. By putting them in camps, they would have to be fed, and the feeding of prisoners at that time would have been a major problem. The Army had suddenly acquired the problem of feeding the German Army as well as itself. The German Army's captured supplies were used, but it took time to get the supplies to the right places.

★ ★ ★

When in Munich (Munchen in German), there was a pile of bricks and rubble that had been Hitler's Beergarden. Munich looked like all the rest of the German cities, in that it was just a bunch of smashed buildings with people going here and there. Fred wondered why they were going in any direction at all because he could see no place for them to go.

★ ★ ★

For three and a half years Fred had been vitally interested in the war, but now it was finished. All the time there was something to be done, and as he looked around all he could see was the smashed country and wonder why it was all necessary. Of course, the answer was self-evident. If we had not done it, Hitler would have done it to us. He asked himself, "Why?" Many lives had been lost, homes and buildings destroyed. He certainly wanted to get home again and live a free and civilized life.

★ ★ ★

In May of 1945 the Wing took over a nice home that was quite modern and very complete. It did not have many sleeping rooms. That was soon fixed by changing over the rooms that were not originally designed for sleeping. When buildings or houses were needed, the MG (Military Government) was told that a certain place was wanted. The owners were told to be out by a certain time, usually the next day. Then we were able to have the property.

★ ★ ★

When in France, it was said that the Germans did not believe in double beds. Fred found out that the story was correct because he did not see any double beds. What they had were single beds, placed next to one another so that they looked like one big bed. They were even made to fit tight with the ends doweled. In the place he just left, he saw one pair of beds made so that the left side of one and the right side of the other were curved. The connecting inside edges were flat, straight and placed tight together. It looked as if the German people just pretended they didn't sleep double.

★ ★ ★

Fred found a waffle iron in one of the cupboards. It was not an electric one but one that worked on a stove. He got some flour, eggs and butter from the mess and decided they all should have some waffles. He located a German, who spoke English and also ran the enlisted men's tavern, and asked him if he could get him a recipe for waffles. He had one right there. Fred then had to get some baking powder from the mess, as well as some milk. He made some syrup from white sugar by caramelizing it and adding water. Colonel Rhea brought out a can of fig preserves that tasted great, and they all ate waffles.

★ ★ ★

The Major had planned on going to Army Headquarters but decided not to go because he could not get a jeep until about 2:00 in the afternoon. The following day he wished that he had gone the day before. His clerk went to Army Headquarters with the courier just for the ride. He left about 2:30. He came back the next morning and said that, while he was there, General Von Runstadt, who had been captured with all his staff, was brought in and the clerk had a good look at him. The General and his staff were dressed in their very best. All of our officers, including the General, whose division had captured him, were dressed in their combat uniforms.

★ ★ ★

While in France, it was heard that it was the policy of the Germans for the women to bear as many children as possible and that a medal was given to women who had four or more. Also, if a woman was not having children by her husband, she was required to live at the quarters of the SS troops in an attempt to become pregnant.

Schwabisch Hall

There was another story along the same line. Three officers stayed at the Schwabisch Hall quarters overnight on their way back to their squadrons, after acting as controllers for the support missions of the front line troops. There, they talked to a woman who spoke good English. She told them that it was also the duty of the SS troops to see that all women were pregnant if they were not already, or had not had a child recently. This not only included married women but also included single women who were old enough to bear children. The woman did not mention where her husband was, but the officers found a new German officer's uniform hanging in the closet. Someone had left in quite a hurry. The German government also made it possible for a woman to marry the father of her child after he had been killed in action if he had not already married the girl.

Just before dark, a Cub plane circled over Schwabisch Hall several times and, as far as anyone could tell, left just over the top of the hill, which rose behind the town. Later, there was a call from an airfield which was up on the hill and about a mile away from the crest. The Cub had circled between the airport and the edge of the hill, disappeared and shortly afterward was heard to crash. Captain Weitzel was called. Because he was in the intelligence section, it fell upon him to try to locate the plane. He checked with our own flight section. All of our planes were in, but he thought that it might be someone trying to get in, perhaps injured. Weitzel got a car and started out about 10:00 looking for it, driving all around on the side roads everywhere. He came back about 1:00 a.m. without finding it.

In the morning, right after breakfast, Convery went out with

Captain Stidson to look over the airport which was being repaired because of bombings and also to look for the Cub. Some GIs were located who had both seen and heard the plane and who also could tell us just about where it had gone down. They drove around, found a road leading to the crest of the hill, drove across fields, and generally followed along the edge. They located the plane within about 75 yards of the edge of the hill where it had crash landed in a grassy field. It was a German trainer, with the Swastikas painted out with thin paint that didn't quite cover them up. The plane was in good shape; one wing was cracked up a bit. He had come in with his wheels up and made a belly landing.

A funny thing about the landing was that the farmer of the land had gone out and cut the grass all around the plane and right up to it. Maybe there was a reason. They got an interpreter and grilled the farmer but could get no answer out of him except that he had wanted to cut the grass in that field and had started in that little corner. They thought that maybe he was trying to make it look like the plane had been there for some time. Actually it would have in just a few days, the way the grass was growing at that time of the year. Because they were there early in the morning, he had only enough time to cut one cart load and had not cut one section of grass where the plane had first hit leaving skid marks in the taller grass. In order to find the farmer, they started tracking the cart that had hauled the grass away. Farmers in that part of Germany did not make hay but cut and fed the green grass to their cows and horses.

They found tracks in two different directions leading away from the plane, with the tracks of a heavier load going in the direction from which they had come. They could also tell that the cart had gone in that direction because of the way the grass had bent under the wheels. They followed the tracks to a partial road and noted that the tracks had made shiny tracks on the packed dirt road. They were positive they were on the right course because they saw fresh cow dung.

They tracked the cart into the barnyard through geese, children, chickens and into the barn where they found the cart full of freshly cut grass. By that time another officer, a Captain from a tank destroyer company, quartered in Schwabisch Hall for police purposes, had joined them. He could speak a bit of German and asked for *the herren*, the man. He talked to a little old German lady, who was rather stooped and who tried very hard to pretend that she didn't understand. Finally she directed us into a field where they found the farmer, took him down to the plane and interrogated him there. He had a young fellow with him who apparently worked on the farm.

The young fellow spoke Polish and apparently was a Polish soldier who had been assigned to the farmer. However, he could have been in the plane and used the plane to get home. So, they checked his papers quite carefully. He spoke both Polish and German.

From the field, they went down to the plane and began looking around some more. They found a place where a pointed shovel had been used to take up about a half shovel full of dirt and sod. It had been done before the grass had been cut, or at least before it was raked, because the hole was full of small pieces of grass. Why the one shovel of dirt and sod and no signs of the shovelful? They looked for it but couldn't find it. The farmer said that there had been a piece of shrapnel there, and that was all we could get out of him. Maybe so. There were shell holes around the field, so his story was logical.

Further looking around brought out some tracks in the high grass, leading along the edge of the hill toward a thicket about 200 yards away and toward a small barn. There were a pair of tracks, and since the plane was a two-seated plane, they were positive they were on target. They got to the barn and very carefully investigated but found nothing. The small barn was right on the edge of the hill, overlooking the town, in a small orchard. Behind the barn was a small path leading down the steep hill toward the town. At the end of the orchard were some small buildings which looked inhabitable.

They went to the house and were announced by a small, but very noisy, dog on a leash and wire. A young girl of thirteen to fifteen came out. She was real pretty without the help of dresses or costume. She was blond, her hair pulled back tightly, with a good complexion. She wore a tight yellow sweater that let you know that while she was not quite grown up, she soon would be. She wore not shorts and not bloomers but a black combination of the two that couldn't have been any smaller and yet they were rather full, up high and tight around her legs (cute legs, too), no stockings, of course, and just wooden-soled shoes.

The TD (tank destroyer) officer attempted to speak to her in German, before she asked, "Do you speak English?" They were just about floored. She was then asked whether she had seen anyone the night before, whether she had heard the plane come down, and several other questions. She spoke fairly good English but was stumped on quite a number of words. They had to re-phrase their questions. At first she denied seeing anyone or knowing anything about anyone from the plane, but they got her to admit that she saw two persons. Then she decided that she should get her mother. Her mother came out, and the girl acted as interpreter.

The best that they could get was that two men had left the plane. She went to the window when she heard the dog barking, after hearing the plane come down. She saw them go over the hill toward the path; they were both carrying sacks over their shoulders. It was too dark to be able to tell what kind of uniform they were wearing. She and her daughter were in the house because all persons were required to be inside after 7:00 which was the curfew for civilians. They had been in bed when the plane came down.

That is the end of the story as far as they were concerned because it was the end of the trail for them. The TD officer was looking for them in the town, and in the event they were found, they would be shot because they were up to no good. If they should turn themselves in, nothing would be done, because that was the proper procedure.

Major Convery and Captain Stidson conjectured that the pilot of the plane knew exactly where he was because he circled around several times as though he were looking for some particular spot. He was not in trouble, forcing him to make a crash landing because he had flown toward the airport and could have landed on the runway. There was plenty of runway (concrete) for a Cub to land, and a training plane such as his, similar to a Cub, could land there. His tank had gas in it.

They believed he wanted someone in the town to know he was there because he circled down low several times before disappearing over the top of the hill.

He was a good aviator because anyone wanting to get into the town, as quickly as possible, without being seen on the roads, would drop his ship as close to the edge of the hill as possible and get into the brush immediately, which was exactly what he did. He had to skim right over the tops of the hillside trees and land. Otherwise, he would have gone farther on up the slope and would have been visible to troops at a supply dump a short distance away. As it was, he was out of view. From the edge of the hill or bluff, there was a gentle rise for about 30 yards. The troops were about another 500 yards away.

He knew exactly where the path was, because the tracks headed right for it and not directly over the edge of the bluff. And last, but certainly not least, the TD Captain knew there was a woman living in town whose husband was a high ranking German Luftwaft officer. The whole situation was a mystery that was never solved.

★ ★ ★

On a trip to Brigade Headquarters, Fred had to go by the 44th Infantry Headquarters which was Harry's regiment. He stopped to look up Harry and found that he had missed him by one day. As Athletic Officer for the regiment, he had been sent to a school in Paris to take a course on "Information and Education." So he missed Harry again! Fred was scheduled to go to Paris on the 16th and decided to look him up while there.

★ ★ ★

On 14 May 1945 the roads were still filled with thousands of people who had been released from the concentration camps on their way back to their homes. Most of them wore striped clothing similar to a prison uniform except that the stripes were vertical and were brown and white rather than black and white. Others wore civilian clothing. They were from concentration camps because there was an X painted on each back. That was supposed to be the target in the event they were trying to escape.

★ ★ ★

On a trip in Germany, Majors Scherer from Brigade Headquarters and Convery were on a trip together. Scherer told Convery that an odd order had come through his Headquarters to the effect that there was a place named Buchenwald somewhere in the area where they were traveling at the time. The order stated that no U.S. Army personnel of any rank were to go there under any circumstances. Scherer didn't have any idea what it was all about.

Later on, both learned of the concentration camp and how millions of Jews, other civilians, men, women, and children had been put to death there. The camp had its own crematory for the disposal of bodies, which had a daily capacity of 400. Many atrocities and brutalities were committed against the helpless inmates, such as the tanning of human skin to make lamp shades and book covers.

★ ★ ★

The non-fraternization policy was really getting some of the boys down. The girls found out that Army personnel was prohibited from talking to them. The girls were actually teasing a little bit, because so many of them gave that pleasant smile that said *I would like to talk to you.* It was only natural, because the country was full of women and no men, that is, young men. Nevertheless, to talk to a German, except on official business, was *verboten.* Fred thought a lot of the boys had a pretty good idea about how Adam and Eve felt in the garden of forbidden fruit.

With the war over, everyone had time on his hands, and with the warm weather the rivers and lakes were turning into bathing beaches. The GIs were there in numbers and so were the girls in their none-too-plentiful bathing suits. But the men could not talk to the girls and vice versa. Some of them tried it, resulting in a court-martial. The usual cost was about $65.00.

There was a lot of talk going around regarding who would be going back home and who would be kept there. A point system was worked out and the points were to be used as a basis of comparison. For officers, there were two screenings: first, to determine whether they were surplus to the needs of the theater and, second, to return to the U.S. as surplus, to then determine whether they were essential or non-essential to the Army. Accordingly, they would be reassigned or released. Officers were to be selected as surplus and non-essential by consideration of the factors of military necessity, efficiency and desire to remain in the Service. An adjusted Service rating score similar to that of the enlisted men was to be assigned to each officer.

It all meant that an officer must first be surplus. Next he must be inefficient and then have a service record allowing him to be released from duty. That sort of put an officer on the spot. Before VE day, in order to get released from the Army as an officer, the same regulations more or less applied. He had to be surplus and also inefficient. Fred checked his records and for the last six months of 1944, the General gave him an efficiency rating of "superior."

PART VI

PARIS

Rest & Recreation May 1945

Fred received his R & R (Rest & Recreation) leave for Paris and was able to arrange for a flight in a C-78 (a five-passenger two-door plane). He was positive that he would be able to find Harry as he was to be at the school for ten days. The school was at the University of Paris.

Fred arrived in Paris okay, and the first thing he did after registering for his assigned hotel room was to take the subway to the University of Paris. He located Harry in his classroom, and the instructor released Harry from the class. From that time on Harry and Fred really had a good time. They started out by doing some sightseeing. That night they took in a cabaret. They did some more sightseeing the next day and took in a show that night. Harry stayed with Fred both nights. The first night they really tied one on. Harry took care of Fred, and Fred took care of Harry. Both got back to the room as two nice little boys.

Harry and Fred enjoyed themselves one of the nights visiting the *Champs Elysees*, near the *Arc de Triomphe* (the GIs called the Avenue the "Champs of Elsie"). They came upon hundreds of French people in the large open area of the square. They had formed a huge, dancing circle by holding hands and were chanting *Fini la Guerre, Fini la Guerre*, which meant *end of the war*. Feeling friendly, Harry and Fred joined the chanting circle. With others joining in, it was not long before Harry and Fred became separated, and Fred lost Harry in a crowd of about 1,000. He spent the next hour looking for him before he finally found him. He was sitting on a curb, crying his eyes out, an actual crying jag. The curb was directly under the Arc de Triumph, and right in front of Harry was a large bronze seal set in the concrete pavement. The seal was for the Unknown Soldier of World War I, buried in a tomb under the Arc de Triumph. He persuaded Harry that World War I had been over for about 25 years and that he shouldn't feel so bad for the fellow down there in the tomb even though he was cold. The next day Harry had to return to his school at the University of Paris.

★ ★ ★

While Major Convery was in Paris, he visited all of the various Headquarters of the European U.S. Armies, and they asked him to record the details of the AA operations of the Wing during the invasion of Southern France. They had the procedures of all of the Armies but that particular part had not been written, nor had there been anything recorded from the Early Warning standpoint for an amphibious operation. All the details had to be gotten together with drawings and diagrams.

★ ★ ★

While in Paris, Fred had two tickets for the Follies Bergiere, but at noon he met one of his former AA officers who was on leave and he invited Fred to dinner. He turned the tickets in and got his money back. Lieutenant Boulliett came over as a French liaison officer and had made some very fine French friends. He took Fred to a good French restaurant. The owner used to be one of the leaders of the underground.

On his way back to his hotel Fred was propositioned by a good-looking gal. When he told her he wasn't interested, she offered everything in the books and finally offered an exhibition with her friend. He could only get rid of her by telling her that he only had 300 francs. When he told her that, she left in a hurry to look for someone else. The next morning he flew back to Schwabisch Hall.

★ ★ ★

A USO show came and all were glad to go. It was really a good show although much the same as all the others. The master of ceremonies of this one was really on the ball and they had a lot of good laughs. After the show was over, Lieutenant Colonel Rhea, who lived at the house along with eight other officers, brought up the whole troop—three men, two girls, and the two drivers who chauffeured the show around. One of the girls played an accordion and one of the men played a guitar. It was a lot of fun. Two of the men were brothers and both had been emcees in night clubs. They kept up a continual string of gags. Of course, there was a lot of talking, and soon they began singing. The girl with the accordion, as well as the man with the guitar, entertained them with songs. He could sing a lot of songs inappropriate for a USO show but commonplace in a night club. They brought out what liquor they had and really enjoyed themselves.

When the USO people were at the house, one of the girls saw the bathroom, and when she found out that there was hot water, she made arrangements right away to come back and have a hot bath. She came back with another girl and they spent the better part of two hours in the bathroom. They washed their hair and then asked whether there was any lemon powder around to be used when rinsing their hair. They claimed that it cut the soap, just the same as regular lemon juice. They certainly appreciated the hot water. Traveling around was not fun and it did present its difficulties. We moved a lot and took along everything we needed so that we could go anywhere and get along. But traveling around and depending upon what other people could do for them left them out in the cold many times.

★ ★ ★

The town of Schwabisch Hall was located on a plateau as

well as down in a valley. A main road passed through the valley and wound up to the top of the hill. About halfway up the hill, there was a mound or crosswise hump in the road. All of the military traffic had to use that main road through the town to get to points farther east and south.

One day the engineers decided to remove the bump because it was a nuisance to all vehicles. The road was made of paving brick, and the hump had been paved over as though it always had been there. When they removed the paving brick and bump, the engineers found two bombs, buried there by the Germans, that were armed to explode upon being disturbed by any traffic. No one could guess why the bombs had not exploded.

Bombs in roadway

Fred told Harry Overly about the bombs when he visited in Schwabisch Hall, and Harry said that his entire division had used that road when they were moving on toward Bavaria. Fred had driven over the hump many times himself.

★ ★ ★

A soldier from Headquarters who spoke Polish was in charge

of the workers and was talking to the girls who did the house-work. They told him that before the Americans were there they had to work for a German farmer. They worked in the fields all day and then came back to do the housework. They never got through until after 11:00 at night and were only allowed to eat after that when they were actually too tired to eat.

* * *

We expected to be moving to another location. We were puzzled about what we were going to do with the civilian help. The Poles could go along, but any others had to stay behind. All of the help came from the displaced person's camp, and the military government was trying to get them all back to their own countries as soon as possible. Russia said that the Russians must stay where they were in order to keep track of them, that they could go if they wanted to, but before they left they had to sign a statement relinquishing their Russian citizenship. As a result, they would be forever barred from returning to Russia. If they were to go along with the Army, there would have been a lot of red tape from that time on. They were used as KPs in all units, to keep the buildings clean, to serve as waitresses and housekeepers, and to do anything to help or lessen the work to be done. They were fed, and the government paid them about $8.00 or $9.00 a month. It was not known whether the U.S. paid them or their own government.

* * *

In July, Headquarters moved and the six staff members lived in a home that had been taken over. Two Polish girls were as-signed to the home as housekeepers and lived in the servants' quarters. When the house was seized, the residents were just told to leave and were not able to take their possessions with them. The lady who used to live there came back several times to ask for one thing or another. She was not allowed to go into the house so we would go after them for her.

It certainly was odd to be talking to those people about how the bombers came over. They talked as though the bombers were from some entirely different country than the U.S. They told about how they were warned, etc. The subject was brought up because she wanted a road map that was in the house. One of the maps Fred got for her was a map they used to discern from the radio reports where the bombers were. They told us that they could never do anything with any regularity, that they would often be preparing a meal and not be able to finish the meal because they had to go to the cellar. Or maybe they would be working in the garden and would have to come in. They could never plan to do a thing, even go shopping, because the planes might be coming and they would have to quit and go to a shelter. They did not talk as though they were angry at all, just as a matter of fact and interest. Fred didn't think that he could have felt that way. The things she wanted were some soap that they could not find, some writing paper, toilet paper, a knife, and a few other odds and ends.

The lady living next door wanted to bake us a loganberry pie, but because their ration of lard was only one ounce per week per person, she just couldn't do it.

★ ★ ★

The Major had an Opel to use rather than a jeep. It was a small car and was good to use to make his safety inspections. Being a sedan, it was more comfortable than a jeep. One of the groups under them turned it in because they could not take it with them. They were heading for the staging area to the States and on to the Pacific. There was one problem. We were very short of drivers. We had to send drivers to other units that were short in order that they would be filled up when they left for the staging area. One of the clerks was used as a driver. Doing your own driving was verboten.

PART VII

GOING HOME

August 1945

By 5 August, the chances of Fred starting on his way home were really good. The names of high point officers of the Wing were requested. Within two hours names had to be sent to the 9th Air Force of those officers with a point total over 118 and who were not indispensable. Fred's name was on the list with 133 points.

Some officers were on leave when their orders came through, and in those cases it was just too bad because they were not there to take off. Of course, their names would be submitted in the next quota, usually a month later.

Fred was told in the evening that a phone call had come in with the message that he was on the orders and that he would be leaving in the morning. He had to pack and be ready to leave. The orders were to come in the morning and he expected to take off shortly afterward.

Everybody on orders from the Wing, for return to the States, were flown from Darmstadt to Lebourget Airfield outside of Paris in France. They were billeted in some barracks near there. They remained at Lebourget Airfield until the end of the month when they were transferred to another staging area near Le Harve. During that time they had to be processed and went through a number of tests. They were given smallpox vaccinations, if needed, and that was about all. They were able to go into Paris whenever they wanted to, which was the way they usually spent their time.

On 31 August, they were told about 8:00 in the evening to send all of their hold baggage down to the port. They were to leave at 9:30 in the morning to board ship and head for home.

★ ★ ★

Twenty-eight months earlier, Fred had been wondering what was going to be? Would he get back? Would he ever see his family again? Would he be a whole person? Would he?

Now he knew! He was on his way home!